'Great Teams are made of Great Individuals. I [...] organizations and teams today are not struct[...] of the people who are working in them. This [...] who's serious about the work they do.' **Sir Cl[...] Winning Coach, Director of Sport for Team GB at the London 2012 Olympic Games and Founder, Captured**

'In the world of performance, mindset is ultimately what makes the difference between winning and losing. *Showing Up* will disrupt the way you think while you're working and help you raise your game in the process. Update now!' **Steve Backley OBE, 3-time World Record Holder and 3-time Olympic Medallist**

'Whenever Tim works with us, he provokes something different in our thinking. He gets under the skin of life in a team and yet remains distant enough to point out the things most of us haven't noticed. Just like he does face-to-face, this book asks annoying and provocative questions that will stop you in your tracks and challenge you to think and work differently. We've been on the receiving end and this stuff works.' **Andy Maisey, Regional Director, HSBC**

'Tim's ideas and thinking are inspirational. They have motivated us as an organization to completely change the way we look at how we support people to give all of their self at work and really understand the purpose of their contribution towards our goals. His message is easily accessible and compelling and I've marvelled at how these ideas have grabbed the attention of all our teams, from apprentices to the Boardroom.' **Jerry Clough, Western Locality Managing Director, NEW Devon Clinical Commissioning Group, NHS**

'This book brings together in one place all the critical "hooks" of development that Tim has shared with me over the last few years. If you are looking for simple, memorable and highly effective ways to enhance you, then this is a book to read.' **Jane Hanson, Chief People Officer, Yorkshire Building Society**

'One of the reasons we work with Tim is that he just "gets us". He always challenges our thinking and inspires our store teams in a way that's simple, memorable and do-able. Their feedback has been fantastic.' **Jo Moran, Head of Service, Marks & Spencer**

'Tim offers fresh and accessible perspectives for a new workplace mindset that will inspire you to take greater responsibility for the way you work and the results you get every day.' **Roger Black MBE, Olympic Medallist and World Champion**

'Tim's idea of work being like school with pay is brilliant. It says just about everything, and once you get it, it's impossible to think and operate the same way again. For Tim, *Showing Up* is personal not theory, and his experiences and examples give his message real credibility. This book is spot on for any business or individual that's looking to step things up a level.' **Mike Woolfrey, CEO, 4C Group**

'*Showing Up* nails all the big questions about the meaning of fulfilment at work but also manages to ask some brave new ones that will change the way you think. Transformational.' **Pierre Lever, CEO, Asia for Argus Media Ltd and co-author of 57 Minutes: All That Stands Between You And a Better Life**

'New, practical and hugely relevant perspectives on the realities and pace of the modern workplace, written in a language we can all relate to.' **Maria Bourke, Managing Director, Let's Get Healthy**

'From my own experience of his work, Tim's open and engaging style as a critical partner transfers directly onto the pages of this book. It reads the same way he operates; thought-provoking, direct and yet with a smile on its face. Tim's words always ring in my ears long after he's worked with me and I know the words of this book will do the same for its readers. Recommended.' **Alastair McLellan, Editor, Health Service Journal**

'Refreshing and insightful, *Showing Up* reminds you of your endless potential and tests the evolved wisdoms of corporate life. Tim brings a unique energy and perspective in creating the perfect guide to authentic leadership, whilst avoiding the headmaster ritual. Straight from the university of life, this book is a wake-up call for everyone from first jobbers to CEOs.' **Gary Critchley, Shared Services Senior Manager, AMEA, PepsiCo**

'In *Showing Up*, Tim Robson offers an insightful and inspirational exploration of an issue crucial for the future of work and the workplace. Whether you are just entering the world of work or a hardened veteran, this book should be essential reading.' **Dr. James Bellini, Futurologist, Executive Coach and Director of The Talent Foundation**

SHOWING UP

How to Make a Greater
Impact at Work

TIM ROBSON

CAPSTONE
A Wiley Brand

Registered office
John Wiley and Sons Ltd, The Atrium, Southern Gate, Chichester, West Sussex, PO19 8SQ, United Kingdom

For details of our global editorial offices, for customer services and for information about how to apply for permission to reuse the copyright material in this book please see our website at www.wiley.com.

Wiley publishes in a variety of print and electronic formats and by print-on-demand. Some material included with standard print versions of this book may not be included in e-books or in print-on-demand. If this book refers to media such as a CD or DVD that is not included in the version you purchased, you may download this material at http://booksupport.wiley.com. For more information about Wiley products, visit www.wiley.com.

Designations used by companies to distinguish their products are often claimed as trademarks. All brand names and product names used in this book and on its cover are trade names, service marks, trademark or registered trademarks of their respective owners. The publisher and the book are not associated with any product or vendor mentioned in this book. None of the companies referenced within the book have endorsed the book.

Library of Congress Cataloging-in-Publication Data

Robson, Tim, 1972–
   Showing up : how to make a greater impact at work / Tim Robson.
       pages cm
   Includes bibliographical references and index.
   ISBN 978-0-85708-541-2 (pbk.)
 1. Employee motivation. 2. Teams in the workplace. 3. Work–Psychological aspects.
4. Employees–Attitudes. I. Title.
   HF5549.5.M63R627   2014
   650.1–dc23

                                    2014000619

A catalogue record for this book is available from the British Library.

ISBN 978-0-857-08541-2 (pbk) ISBN 978-0-857-08542-9 (ebk) ISBN 978-0-857-08543-6 (ebk)

Cover design by Salad Creative

Set in 11/14.5 pt Gill Sans Std by Toppan Best-set Premedia Limited
Printed in Great Britain by TJ International Ltd, Padstow, Cornwall, UK

To those who've inspired me, whether standing or fallen.

CONTENTS

INTRODUCTION

Over 3 billion people across the planet showed up for work today. But which version of them arrived at their workplace? Is it one their friends would recognize? How closely will it resemble their job title and description? Is it the same person they'd promised at interview or a version of themselves their family would be proud of?

Many different versions of us show up in the places we work, and for a variety of reasons. Sometimes when we're working, we're really not ourselves.

When I was a child, I always wanted to work in a big office. My father was a civil servant in Central London for most of my childhood and seeing him head off in the morning to an office in the city seemed exciting and glamorous and I thought it was *cool*. I was intrigued about his working life and was convinced that 'the office' was the place for me when I was old enough to get there. My mother tells me I used to play 'business' in our lounge at home, using the coffee table as my desk and taking calls on an old work phone Dad had found for me (these were very important calls, and I was quite successful).

My interest in commercial working environments and the ways people do 'work' together has never left me. I've spent most of my working life in and around large organizations, with their many management layers and structures to engage with. I've seen managers come and go, operating models expand and contract and along the way have witnessed organizations and individuals behaving both brilliantly and disgracefully, sometimes all at the same time. Running my consultancy practice over the last few years has also enabled me to see corporate life through an additional and valuable lens, with the privilege of being part of and yet distant from the clients and teams I'm working with.

For too many companies and the teams that work in them, I've noticed an underlying problem that seems to hold them back. It's not their product mix, sales channels, operating model or the market conditions; it's something often unseen but possibly more impactful.

The underlying mindset and working mentality of the people in an organization goes a long way to defining its culture. And too many organizations feel like being back at school. They're arranged like a school, they operate like a school and the people that work in them every day behave as though they're wearing school uniform and lined up in year groups. The only difference between some of the companies we find ourselves working in and the schools we attended as children, is that at the end of each month we now see a wage arrive in our bank accounts.

Going to work can sometimes feel like school. School, *with Pay*.

When our work is like school, the ways we think and our modes of operating are exactly the same as they were all those years ago, when we wore short trousers and tried to stay awake in assembly. Companies, teams, organizations and people who've signed up to School with Pay are living with operational norms and ways of working that are lifted from the playground and re-establish the classroom. And whether adopted intentionally or entirely by accident, this isn't effective for any of us and will harm us creatively and restrict us commercially.

School with Pay is a workplace mindset that's killing us and it doesn't ... have ... to be this way.

In my own working experience, I've seen what can really be possible when people start Showing Up in their fullness in all of the work they do. The results are amazing, and yet sadly these environments and the people working in them can too often find themselves on the fringes of the larger machines they're part of and with a corporate brain that doesn't understand the depth of what's being created. School with Pay can mean that Showing Up rarely lasts long enough to be more than 'a moment in time', destined to one day become a memory rather than growing into an ongoing reality. Working environments where people *really* show up seem fragile and appear somewhat skittish, at risk of their own existence and eventually prey to the upward food chain of centralized operating standards.

I've become increasingly troubled and frustrated by what I've seen happening around me. Something's wrong when the cultural norms and practices of a business seem able to take alive, colourful and creative individuals and over time induce standardization and fear, with personal power often handed on a plate to the most important person in the room.

When we head off to work but don't Show Up, something's broken in our collective thinking.

Thankfully, Apple's iPhone changes everything. I don't mean the device itself (although I'd probably recommend it). The game-changer for all of us is in three short words that appear on our screens occasionally:

Updates are Available.

Three words and a simple invitation prompted the reflections and discovery that resulted in the book you're reading. Showing Up is an *update* to the way we think, react and operate in the work we do and the places where we do it. We'll look at the paradigms that underpin the School with Pay mindset and create some alternatives that are refreshingly powerful. Showing Up is what happens when our mindsets and surrounding conditions mean we bring the very best of ourselves to the work that we do, with no filters, no checks, no doubts and no last minute adjustments necessary. It's what happens when we choose to 'leave school' in the ways that we're operating and loosen the school ties of the patterns in our thinking.

When we Show Up, time seems to work differently. It runs slower, or faster, it stands still or we lose track of it. We laugh and smile more than at other times, even if we're under pressure. Once we truly understand the immense value and potential of every person in our organizations, then maybe we can take that potential seriously enough to allow it to take its place, on display, public and without apology for the whole world to experience. *This* sort of working doesn't feel like work and often means we have more energy than ever.

The opportunity to show up can be there for all of us, in any job, in any organization and in any part of the world in which we find ourselves. 'Work' can be amazing, adrenaline-filled, muscle-stretching and full of possibility, regardless of the sector we're in. And if you allow this book to spark an update in your own working mindset, the same invitation could change the way *you* view your professional life and transform your performance in the process.

Welcome to the App Store for new workplace thinking — here's to three words, their invitation and the start of your own journey ...

Now Show Up!

Tim Robson
Stratford upon Avon, UK
2014

UPDATES ARE AVAILABLE

What does it mean to start Showing Up? To get there, we need Icebergs, Butterflies, Bath Plugs and Grade School. But first, Smartphones.

If you've got a smartphone, grab it and open up the equivalent of your device's App Store. How many updates do you have available, Right Here, Right Now?

How many applications, that you downloaded previously, have since been updated? Improved, re-developed, refreshed and reanimated versions are available now, although you can't experience them, because you're still running the old versions.

How many updates did you have? 1, 3, 10, more than 15?

Maybe you didn't get round to it.

Maybe it wasn't a priority.

But where else might that be happening in your life?

Which old versions of yourself are still loaded on your system?

Which aspects of your thinking need upgrading, in a world that's changing and for the person you're becoming?

In your professional life, what beliefs and methods that maybe worked for you previously are now obsolete, in today's market or for tomorrow's opportunities?

A client once told me their outstanding updates went into three figures but that they'd run out of space to install them due to the 'junk apps' already loaded on their device. A junk app is one you don't use anymore, or you forgot you downloaded, but none-theless is sitting there, taking up your memory. Imagine if you knew your work-life could change, but you'd have to remove what was getting in the way or discard some things that were no longer relevant. You probably already know what junk you're still carrying with you.

When we buy an app, it's not just about the 99c or 69p we spend today. It's about the deal within the deal. We're not just buying this version of the app; we're also buying into its future and the versions that are to come. The underlying assumption is that the current version will at some point be updated. Apps are destined to change and are always in development. They'll *never* be completed and are *always* works in progress.

Apps mirror life, because you and me and everything is always changing.

We update various aspects of our lives on an ongoing basis. We change our footwear and our hairstyles, we refresh the colour of the walls in our houses and trade up technology. We even upgrade our wardrobes (some of us) as fashions change and new looks emerge that we buy into.

So why don't we update our professional mindsets as often as we change the cars we drive?

The way we think and operate at work can resemble a trusted pair of comfortable shoes; old and tired, but too hard to let go of. For some of us, our outlook on work and life, work-life and life-work is in serious need of a refresh.

Thinking this way, the descriptions of an App update's features and benefits make interesting reading:

IMPROVEMENTS:
'now you can ... we've added these great new features ... now updated to include ... a completely refreshed view ...'

FIXED ISSUES:
*'fixes possible crashes ... resolved issue with ... (and my personal favourite) ... **improved stability** ...'*

Which improvements and new features for the way you work might be available to you?

What issues and glitches that you've lived with for years could finally be fixed?

Where do you need to improve your *professional* stability?

You and I are remarkably-designed individuals and our mindset, patterns of thinking, behaviours and responses to the world around us are like apps that are running on our body's amazing hardware. We're not static creations, finished or perfected and with all our talents developed and maximized.

We're an idea, a suggestion and a glimpse of potential.

Today's version of yourself won't be sufficient to meet the demands of tomorrow. Yesterday's thinking is already out of date. And the beauty and mystery of the human mind is that we're designed to work like this – we're hard-wired to change, through the environments we find ourselves in and the circumstances we encounter. Our natural capacity for development and evolution is immense; the very essence of life is that we change over time. Wherever you find yourself today and at whatever stage of your life or career you've reached, your software still has room for development. You're designed to be updated, not built for completion. Today's version of you can be better, do better, feel better and be refreshed … if you're prepared to let it.

The updates we need often emerge naturally. As we rub shoulders with the world, our experiences shape us, new perspectives change us and we're no longer the people we used to be. Our software becomes outdated. Functionality that once seemed super-fast can begin to feel slow and our bodies occasionally tell us this is happening – feelings of stress, an unease with how things are and an instinct that life could and should be different are all indicators that you might need an update or are ready for a refresh …

Updating your apps sometimes changes everything. But when life moves so fast, we can forget to return to our App Stores. Updates might be available; new features, patches and critical fixes might be ready to go, but we have to install them and so can choose, of course, to leave things as they are. We can browse our App Store, view breakthrough updates and still decide to leave. And like the badge on the App Store icon that still shouts for our attention, opportunities for improvement will continue to catch our eye as we go about working life. Familiar, repeated and often-visited issues will remind us there might be another way of working, our gut-feel and instincts will prompt us to think about making a change … but we have to make the first move. The work of a developer counts for nothing until you and I accept their offer.

'Updates are Available' is a whispered Invitation.

One newly-released update described itself as 'a fully re-designed app that is invigorated, alive, bolder and better than ever before.' Imagine if you could install that version of yourself at work, today. I bet it would be amazing.

Another said 'in this update we addressed FREQUENT FEED-BACK from our users'. How many colleagues respond to feedback on their style and performance by saying *'oh yeah, loads of people have mentioned that before'* or *'funny, you're not the first person who's said that's a problem'*? Maybe you've said the same things yourself. What updates do you need, to address frequent feedback from your colleagues, your boss or maybe your stakeholders?

The default apps that run in the companies we're part of can give our whole sense of 'work' a bad name. Some people suggest we reject the corporate environment as if it's beyond help or improvement. Walk along the street of any busy town or city at lunchtime and you'll hear hard-working people talking about their job and describing the impact it's having on their lives, their loved ones and their sense of well-being. Often the conversation has a negative vibe. Some people talk about leaving their job as soon as they're able, to head off and create a new future, because 'they just can't be themselves around here ...'.

I'm not so sure. It's easy to criticize something that isn't working. But what if it's not broken, simply an old mindset? Old versions can still work. They're just, well, *old*. It's the equivalent of using Microsoft Word 1.0 on an old PC, loaded by floppy disk. It might still work today and if it did, could help produce documents. But Word 1.0 would be easy to criticize. It would be obvious that some aspects don't provide what you need these days from that sort of software. But Word in itself isn't wrong as a solution – you'd just be working with a really outdated version.

I think the work you and I do can be remarkable and fulfilling, world-changing and side-splittingly fun. Work can be so good that we lose track of time. We just need the right apps to be running.

This book takes a visit to the App Stores of our workplace mindsets and invites us to Update. It suggests improvements we can make, issues that can be fixed and a few new features that could improve our stability. Think of it as a Time-out for you, your team or your company. Time-outs get called to assess where we are in the game, to take a breather and re-group, or to open up a tactical advantage.

Time-outs aren't about leaving the game.

Showing Up is a workplace time-out because there's a game in play, *now*, and because we all spend too many hours working to continue with an approach that isn't successful. A few of us *know* some things need to change ... and a few adjustments might be just what's needed to tip us into a whole new level of performance and possibility.

My hope is to disrupt your thinking, press pause on your hamster-wheel and spark a discussion. I'm convinced that when we start Showing Up, our workplaces could change forever.

Updates are Available. Always. For all of us.

Update now?

Interestingly, IOS 7, the 2013 update to Apple's mobile operating system, included an optional 'auto-update' feature, meaning app updates can now be installed as soon as they become available. I love that. Imagine being the most up-to-date version of yourself in the world, with all your improvements firing and the latest patches doing their good work as soon as you open your eyes every morning. A refreshed you, every day. What would it take for us to all live like that?

Note: while auto-updates is a very cool feature, it's slightly annoying in the context of my metaphor. See what I mean? Even this first chapter might already need updating ...

PAY ATTENTION. KEEP THE PLUG OUT.

Central Periphery Tension

When I started driving as a bullish seventeen-year-old, my first long-awaited lessons were, let's say, tricky. I wasn't a great learner driver. On finally getting behind the wheel of my learner car, I froze. I took lessons during lunch breaks from my first office job, only to return to my desk after every fraught hour with the back of my shirt drenched in sweat and my instructor probably regretting his career choice. He was hard-nosed and experienced, with a good reputation and strong pass-rate record, and on just my second lesson and in a fit of frustration he declared that I had 'Central Periphery Tension'. This essentially meant that when driving down an open road, I stared rigidly at the end of the car rather than the tarmac ahead of me. With clammy fingers gripping the steering wheel and sweat running down my back, I found myself staring at the end of the bonnet as I pressed the accelerator. Just staring.

Central Periphery Tension is a poor strategy for driving. It's high risk on relatively straight roads, but the stakes get higher when turning into traffic from a busy T-junction. Don't try it yourself, but next time you're driving, imagine heading across a lane of traffic to join a road running 90 degrees to you, while all the time staring, hard, at a point two metres directly ahead of you ...

When we drive, we look everywhere *but* the end of our car bonnet and the faster we drive, the further ahead on the road we look. When we're at a T-junction, roundabout or motorway junction, our eyes glance all over the place; checking our mirrors, assessing the road ahead and looking out for what other drivers are doing that we might need to take account of (or at least they should do).

You can't pass your driving test with Central Periphery Tension. In fact, you can't do many things effectively if you're staring right ahead of you.

Thankfully, my CPT dissipated as I became more confident behind the wheel and my instructor's first-time pass-rate was intact at the end of my learning process, but this same learning reaction resurfaced in France over twenty years later when I learned to ski. As I stood nervously on the beginners' slopes, I stared directly at the end of my skis, willing them into submission the same way I had my learner car all those years ago.

Except this time it was different. Rather than getting frustrated and declaring CPT or an alternative accusatory condition, the super-cool Fabian (ski instructors are *always* super-cool) touched me on the arm and offered a couple of lines that have lived with me ever since:

> 'Teeeeam, you're on holiday. Look **up**.
> Where your Attention is, is where you'll Go.'

When I lifted my eyes, I suddenly took in everything I'd managed to ignore while my focus had been on my skis and all my concentration on what seemed a challenging task ahead of me. Around me was the breath-taking vista of the Alps in winter, with Mont Blanc glistening over my shoulder. Around me was the result of everything I'd worked for that year in order for the family to head off to the snow together for the first time. Alongside me were fantastic and treasured friends, who'd encouraged us to ski for years and who'd be with us in what would become one of the most significant and memorable holidays we'd ever had. And all I'd noticed were the end of my skis.

How often at work do we forget to **Look Up**? When our focus is on our tasks and schedule or objectives and responsibilities, we all miss perspectives, delete ideas and ignore opportunities that might be all around us, if we could *just* raise our eye-line slightly and look **up** at what's around us.

When you stare straight ahead of you, it's easy to ignore the broader frame for where you find yourself.

Look Up and Gain Perspective

Think about the job you do today; the environment, the people, the responsibilities, the things you're on the hook for and the rhythm that you're working to.

Now pan back. Take a wider angle. How did you end up doing your current job? How does it support other important aspects of your life and your journey and growth as an individual in the world? What possibilities and advantages does your job bring in your current circumstances?

Pan back a little further. How does *this* job fit in the story of the last 5 or 10 years of your life? What role might it play in the next 10 or 20? Where does today fit in the context of your history and what does it support in relation to your future? Stay here with your thoughts for a while.

Now flick back to today's job and the things you 'have to get done' by the end of this week. Glance at your inbox. Today's 'pressing' issues appear a little smaller, seem less significant and are a component of a broader story, rather than filling your thinking. They're important, but not all-consuming. Necessary, but not life-defining.

Look Up. Where you are might be the result of everything you've worked for.

Where Your Attention Is, Is Where You'll Go

When you ski down anything more challenging than a nursery slope, a key aspect is picking the spots you plan to ski towards; random points some distance away on the slope below you. You navigate a path to them by traversing the mountain, making smooth turns across the slope, and by shifting your weight from one leg to the other, regulating your speed as you pull out of each turn. A competent skier's attention brings their body position, legs and hips into alignment and they all work together to reach the point they identified. A busy piste at the height of the season is littered with skiers pausing on the slopes, reviewing their progress, assessing the conditions and traffic below them and deciding on their next spot to head to, before repeating the process to the bottom of the run.

Whatever your level and regardless of the conditions, you don't drive by peering over the end of your bonnet. And you can't get down a mountain by looking at the end of your skis. Trust me, I've tried to do both.

Your mindset and attention at work is determining where you're headed. Deepak Chopra puts it another way: 'What you give Attention to, Grows.'

If you give attention to Anger, it will grow. If you give attention to Bitterness, it will increase. And so if you choose to give attention to Positivity, it will grow inside you and create a filter through which you view life around you and will define your reactions as you go about your business. And the opposite will, of course, also be true.

Whether driving a car, skiing a mountain, creating a life or building a business, the Buddhist saying rings true – 'What we Think, we Become.'

Attention defines destination.

Attention defines what grows.

Attention defines what gets sifted and what remains.

I realized something that day, on the side of that mountain. As individuals or organizations, our patterns of thinking have established our direction; where our mindset and attention have been is where we've ended up. Think about where you live today, the job you do, your domestic situation and the friends and family you spend your time with.

How many of your answers can be linked in some way to the attention you've given to those aspects of your life?

Where your attention has been (and equally where it hasn't), will have significantly impacted your current circumstances and where in life and work you find yourself.

If this is true for you, it's true for your organization. The only question is whether that thinking and attention is working for you or helping your company and serving to create the right environment for any of us.

- What are you looking at? Where has your **attention** been recently and where has it taken you?
- What's growing in you right now? What are you **becoming**, as a result of your thinking?
- What changes in your **thinking** might be needed to create a different outcome?

If our attention determines our direction, and what we focus on defines where we find ourselves, today's working environment and the way our professional lives are developing reflect our mindsets and the patterns of our thinking. All of which takes us to Icebergs.

The Iceberg Dynamic

There's more to an iceberg than the parts we can see. As little as 10 percent might be above the surface, with 90 percent below; hidden, unseen and yet providing stability and structure for all that's on display.

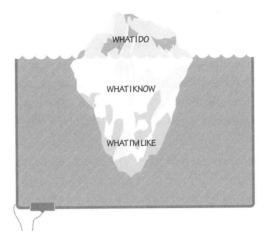

Figure 1: The Iceberg Dynamic

Just like us.

In our working lives, we're Icebergs in the oceans of the organizations we work in. Cultural protocols and norms of behaviour, operational conventions and the ways we operate together all contribute to the environments that surround every one of us while we're working. The extent that our skills, talent, character and potential are visible will depend on the conditions we work in and our responses to what's happening around us.

Water is the most powerful force in nature. And in organizations, it's our working culture and reactions; what I call our Working Mindset.

Take a look at the Iceberg diagram in Figure 1. It describes three simple levels of what's 'on display' for ourselves and the people we're working with.

Process – what I do

This is literally the tip of our Iceberg, with little more than name, rank and serial number on show. We do our job and fulfil our responsibilities but offer little beyond the work required of us and none of our personality. We work the same way as we introduce ourselves in large meetings: 'I'm Tim and I process invoices.'

If you've ever been served in a restaurant by someone working only from What I Do, you'd remember it (if you stuck around long enough): show table, give menu, take order, deliver meal, hand bill. Done.

Hint: Best not to choose a life partner from someone at this level.

Knowledge and Competencies – How I do what I do

As well as doing *what* we do, at this level our expertise and skill is now on display – *how* we do what we do. We apply our knowledge and experience to the table and so move beyond simply completing tasks. People operating from *how* I do what I do will have higher levels of self-awareness and can work alongside others with differing skills to deliver an outcome.

This *person in the restaurant does all the things from the prior level but with far more polish; they're efficient and expert in the way that they serve us, they can answer our questions and could recommend something from the menu.*

Personality and Behaviours – Why I do what I do

The bottom of our Iceberg includes all that has been seen before, but now what we're *really* about is on display; our passions, our beliefs and the things that motivate us. The world's getting far more of us than simply tasks and our knowledge and so can connect with our personality and character. And when aligned with a business goal or outcome, we finally bring all that we've got to the table.

*This person will use all of their talents and skills to make us repeat customers and with energy, knowledge and personality work to create a great experience. They'll be informed, passionate, friendly and above all **fully present** for as long as they're hosting us. We'll probably stay longer, spend more and almost certainly visit again. And we'll tip.*

Just as a regular ocean is affected by tides and the moon, the way a business executes its decisions, manages change, treats its people and serves its customers will all impact the working mindset of the individuals who work in it and how much of them remains on show. The way it handles success and failure. How it manages conflict and competition. Every change programme. Every decision. Every email, appraisal, team meeting or corridor conversation. In fact, everything that happens in our places of work will impact in one way or another the working mindset at play in all of us and the level of the ocean in which our Icebergs sit. The way we operate and do what we do will either drain the ocean that builds around us or will cause a blockage and keep the water-level rising. Like water in a bath tub, life in a business is either Plug Out or Plug In.

Plug In refers to circumstances or environments that mean we show *less* of ourselves at work. They have the effect of putting the plug in, meaning the water-level around us rises and less of our personal Iceberg is visible to the outside world.

Plug Out refers to an environment or working experiences where we show *more* of ourselves through the work we do. They pull the plug *out*, dropping the water-level around us and showing more of who we are to the people that we're working with.

And whether the Plug's out or locked in will determine what our working world experiences of us.

Think about it. What day-to-day aspects of a business or team see the water-levels around us rising, such that colleagues and customers will see less of our Icebergs and a reduced version of all we can offer? What sorts of things do the opposite, draining the water around us and placing more of our knowledge and talents on display and therefore available to apply in the situations we find ourselves in?

I've described the Iceberg Dynamic to many clients over the years and asked them to describe the different Plug Out and Plug In factors at work in their organization. Their answers are always consistent:

PLUG IN (water-level rises)

Lack of Direction	Lack of Trust	Lack of Control
Politics	Inertia	Hierarchy
Standardization	Silence	Uncertainty
Fear	Poor Communication	Rules & Politics
Control	Lack of Time	Confusion
Busy-ness	Blame	Being Ignored
Short-Termism	Isolation	Disempowerment

PLUG OUT (water-level drops)

Clarity	Freedom	Authority
Feeling Valued	Fun/Team Spirit	Choice

Trust	Momentum	Autonomy
Teamwork	Belief	Support
Acknowledgement	Being Known	Interest & Attention
Empowerment	Ideas	Development
Responsibility	Honesty	Celebration
Understanding	Respect	Involvement

- Which words best describe your current working environment?
- Which category do you find yourself spending most time in?
- What reactions are you having to the situations around you and how are they impacting your own personal water-level?
- If you manage people or a team, what decisions have you taken recently that pulled their Plug **Out**? What have you done to enable them to bring more of themselves to work when engaging with colleagues and maybe your customers?
- How might you have put the Plug **In** for your people? What activity have you overseen that could have increased their water-level and mean they brought less of themselves to work?
- Who's working in shallower or deeper waters today than they were a month ago, under your leadership?

As individuals, our 'water-levels' are constantly impacted by the Plug Out or Plug In factors around us.

And if we're leaders or members of a management team, we're creating these factors for the people we're responsible for on a daily basis. We all influence whether our Plugs get pulled.

While the leadership and culture of a large organization might define the dominant culture of a workplace, it's often our own patterns of thinking and behaving within them that make our personal water-levels move in one direction or another. And the level you're working in today will be a defining factor in your current performance.

Our brains are already 70 percent water – we don't need any more pumping in up there. Have you ever felt as though you were getting close to drowning?

Where's your Water-line?

Think about the Iceberg and everything you can bring to a team or company; not just the job you can *do* but also all your knowledge, competencies, personality and behaviours and the possibilities for your performance and contribution when all those gifts and talents are brought together ...

- Maybe you're a great trouble-shooter or calm under pressure.
- Perhaps you're gifted in analysis or cutting through the noise to identify the real issues.
- Maybe you're super-sharp, with instincts that can spot commercial opportunities others don't think of.
- Maybe you're an awesome coach and an excellent listener or always a breath of fresh air in the office.

Now recall the times when you performed or delivered your very best work – the times when you *know* that you nailed it and made a tangible contribution in your team or business (one of those occasions when you lost track of time).

You're allowed to brag to yourself for a moment here. No-one else is listening.

- What did you contribute? What skills did you bring? What talents did you display?
- What were the conditions in which you did what you did?
- Where was your water-line at that exact moment?

When we do our best work, we operate from the bottom third of our Icebergs. The surrounding conditions and our working mindset mean the best of us is on show. Which leads us to a different sort of question:

What proportion of last week did you spend doing, being and bringing those very same things in your current job? Think about your schedule for next week – what opportunities have you created to bring those gifts and talents to the table?

How much of your work-time are you spending at your BEST?

More than 80 percent? Less than 50 percent? Less than 20 percent?

The chances are good that what you identified as 'you at your best' are the same sorts of things you sold us at interview, or when you went through a process for an internal promotion. In interviews, our focus is to show the best of ourselves and so along with a few decent questions from an interviewer, our water-level will be running deep into the bottom third of our Icebergs. We'll provide examples from every aspect of our professional experience, recall compelling life-stories that demonstrate multiple competencies and all the while ensure that our full personality comes across.

Job offers are given to the version of ourselves that we took to the interview. **Did that same version turn up last week, in the job that it landed you?**

What do all your answers so far in this section tell you about your present and personal water-line? If this book does its job, it'll pull your Plug a little bit.

Stories that Show the Madness

We've seen how the Apps that are running on our hardware, where our attention is and the water-levels surrounding us define how much of us Shows Up in our jobs and the work we do. Strangely, the underlying working mindset of people in an organization isn't something we seem to prioritize. Our workplaces tend to be driven by all the things we're busy *doing* and so we struggle to pause occasionally and consider how we're *thinking* and the impact it's having on our group or team results. When I'm working with a client organization, one question loops in my mind as I interact with different teams and people:

What working mindset is in play around here, to have created these outcomes in a business, a division, a team or an individual?

The examples below describe scenarios I'm directly aware of. Your job is to imagine the mindsets behind the outcomes they've created:

...a hedge fund backed group with a £200m+ turnover appoints a new CEO, who kicks off a 'business discovery', asking each divisional head to submit a trading summary at the end of each week. The email and phone lines quickly grow heavy with traffic, as **Managing Directors of £5–10m companies contact each other to see which font they should use on their individual submissions ...**

...a company with a UK-wide network and £100m+ operating budget holds its annual conference, with its top 200 leaders present. The most contentious issue of the event is **finalizing the seating plan for the pre-conference dinner around the preferences of the most senior delegates ...**

...a growing IT service provider moves into new premises following a period of growth, with a goal to double its turnover to circa £12m. The business development director now spends over 10 hours each week **managing issues relating to the organization's car space policy and parking arrangements ...**

...a cost-saving 'initiative' means that executives with responsibility for thousands of people are unable to book their business travel and accommodation unless it is authorized in advance by an executive at board level. Signatory board members have little or no understanding of the context or even the identity of **the many individual submissions they now receive in their inbox every week ...**

Do these scenarios seem familiar to you? Have similar ones emerged in your own workplace?

To create these outcomes, *where must our attention have been?*

Where did we all go?

What Apps must be running (and can we get a refund)?

When we read examples like this in black and white, they seem ridiculous. But each one is real and there are many, many more that I'm sure you could think of in your own environment or experience. In the life of any organization, behaviours evolve and protocols 'develop' and we're often too close to the detail to realize how crazy things have become.

How did we get here? The madness we read is a result of our mindset, whether as individuals or corporately as organizations. Where our heads have been has created these outcomes, which are happening now and yet are surely a distortion of what we all know is really possible.

Why does this sort of thing happen? Why do we allow it? Why doesn't somebody say or do something?

I recently worked with an organization where the CEO had made a few throwaway statements at an executive meeting which someone took seriously and to the letter, immediately kicking off a programme of activity in the company that the CEO was, of course, completely unaware of, oblivious to what they'd accidentally endorsed. Project teams were formed, budgets were agreed and activity was launched with little clarity and even less direction but with a resolute focus on delivering something 'very important, very fast' ... because the CEO 'wanted it to happen'. I wonder if he and his shareholders ever found out what he'd inadvertently started and where else this sort of behaviour was being copied in their company. More worrying of course is the fact that the costs associated with this sort of organizational response were unlikely to be scrutinized closely enough to ensure they're not repeated; next week, next month or maybe tomorrow.

Where was this corporation's attention, and where were they headed?

If our outputs are wrong, we need to correct the thought processes and patterns of attention that created them. Life in an organization doesn't have to mirror the examples above and our workplaces can do better than reducing everything to the lowest common denominator. Yet sadly I'm picking up stories like these more and more regularly. We ignore them in our busy-ness and deflect them with initiatives, but if our underlying mindsets for the way we do our work remain broken, we'll always reach the wrong destination, delivering something that falls short of our best efforts, disappoints our customers and prevents our organization from fulfilling its true commercial potential and impact.

Here's a final example which again demonstrates thinking that restricts us but which we're failing to recognize. During a recent visit to a regular coffee shop in Central London, two people sat down behind me and their conversation was compelling. She led the small-talk and he seemed to agree with whatever she said to him; I guessed her to be the boss and, whoever he was, he seemed completely on-edge. So far, so normal; another coffee-house 'meeting' on another morning in another city. The boss got down to business:

OK, well I thought we should talk now, because I'm not going to be about much after this week blah blah ... we're all so busy right now that we probably won't be able to spend much time with you blah blah ... for the first couple of weeks you'll be on your own blah

*blah … you'll just have to ask us questions in order to get going and
then we'll know how good you are blah blah … we're the sort of
business where everyone's watching, so you'll know pretty quickly
what's not working out blah blah … oh, and we can't give you
a Blackberry, but you'll probably be getting emails in the
evenings – how set up are you for that?*

Each time she paused, he simply nodded, saying 'oh yeah, yeah'
and with every answer his voice got higher and higher. He was
on auto-response, clearly hoping to persuade her that he wasn't
fazed by anything she'd said or had asked him.

Eighty percent of the conversation was led by the boss and
focused on deadlines, targets and how 'everyone was watching'.
It had now become clear why he appeared to be so edgy – this
was obviously his first day on the job. This was his *introduction* to
a new firm and line manager, the *first* experience of his immediate
working future and a reasonable indication of what it would be
like to work around there.

This was his welcome. And he was on the back foot from the
get-go. At no point did the boss acknowledge what had landed
him the job in the first place; at no point did she welcome him
or describe what she thought he'd uniquely bring to the table –
she was less than 20 percent engaged and only just present on
a physical level. And yet he was *utterly complicit* – following her
lead without any question, mirroring her behaviour in the hope
of making a good impression and laying a dangerous foundation
for this particular relationship going forward. In just a few short
moments, he'd entirely lost himself in order to do what he
thought was necessary to survive in the environment this particular boss was creating.

Was this it? Really?

As I left the coffee shop that day, I got to thinking about the meeting I'd just witnessed. What working mindset was in play in those individuals, to have created the interaction that I'd just witnessed? What sort of working relationship was this going to be and how would their company culture be developing?

Cut to the present day.

How many other meetings are happening just like this in coffee shops and break-out areas across the same city *today*, or across the UK, or the entire planet ...? Where else are the bosses spouting, while subordinates agree, and where have we seen this sort of subservience before?

Where else does the 'smaller' person's head drop and simply agree with the higher authority in the room?

It's something about a chalk board, a playground, short trousers and a register ...

SCHOOL WITH PAY –
FIVE PARADIGMS TO BREAK

All of us attended school at some point, and after varying stages and levels of formal education, we left, to head out into the big wide world and into adult working life.

Or did we? Is your job still like school, with pay?

If School with Pay describes our mindsets and collective attention, could it be that when it comes to work and the jobs we do, we exited the school building, but didn't really 'leave'? Could it be that the protocols, behaviours and reactions we experience in our day jobs are simply a replica of behaviours and structures we learned back at school?

In situations with these ways of thinking, your Boss is the Teacher. Their Boss is the Principal. And everyone else is a student, with the same insecurities, fears and reactions we had back in grade school. And if we're a boss, but at school playing teacher, maybe *we're* recreating the classroom for our teams and the people trying to work in them.

We're supposed to have left school, years ago.

What we can see in the stories from the previous chapter is what happens in an organization when School with Pay becomes rampant. It can take root almost anywhere, revealing itself across multiple sectors, industries and cultures and stopping those complicit in it from Showing Up through the work they do. Where this way of thinking exists and in companies where it's thriving, I find deep frustration in individuals and teams, working under unnecessary personal restrictions and in environments with an unnecessary emphasis on power and control. Some organizations and individuals *know* their collective mindset isn't working, but are simply running too fast to generate alternatives, as another crisis lands for them to urgently attend to ...

Outdated mindsets waste valuable time and cause organizations to miss opportunities for innovation and growth. Long-standing and well-known operational flaws and failures remain unresolved when school-yard relationships and childish patterns of thinking get transferred to an adult commercial environment.

School with Pay is dysfunctional; it's old software and flawed thinking and will always hold us back from showing the very best of ourselves.

And updates to our thinking are *always* available.

But what exactly is School with Pay and where does it come from? I believe there are five dominant paradigms that create its mentality and set its direction. We were each taught to think like this a very long time ago. Understanding these will help us develop an update to each of them that will transform our mindsets and mean Showing Up becomes our new way of operating:

1. **Teacher Knows Best**
2. **Do What You're Told**

3. Don't Answer Back
4. Don't Copy
5. (Play Nicely and) Stay out of Trouble.

We were introduced to the five paradigms on our first day at school. Our parents told us first and they were repeated by our teacher ... and repeated ... and repeated ... and repeated, until we got them in the muscle. And stuff that's in the muscle can be hard to unlearn.

*'This is how things **are** round here, children. This is how the world works.'*

Each of the five paradigms is, on the surface, reasonable – for young children starting out in the world. The key thing to understand is that they aren't designed to be permanent. In fact, they're entirely inappropriate for working, professional adults and the cut and thrust of today's commercial environments. Imagine a butterfly trying to fly, with its cocoon along for the ride. It wouldn't be pretty and the butterfly wouldn't be very effective at being what it was born to be. In fact, it probably wouldn't last very long at all.

Cocoons are strange and magical constructions. And they *always* give way to something better. Our formative years at school and the five paradigms were a cocoon for our development, providing the framework for our thinking before we emerged into the world as young adults. And just as a caterpillar's cocoon is eventually jettisoned, school is designed to be discarded when its purpose has been served – and it's not a place we're supposed to return to. And yet, this is *exactly* what happens when, rather than leaving school and heading off into our futures, we retain its constructs and carry its cocoon around in the world with us. With an out-of-date mindset weighing heavy on our brains, it's little wonder our professional lives don't always work out as expected.

School with Pay keeps your thinking restricted, your ideas squashed and your creativity stunted, leaving you ill-equipped for professional life and your potential for growth and adventure.

Have you ever felt restricted or squashed in the job that you do?

Have you ever felt like the walls of your work were closing in on you and that you were banging your head against them?

You and I weren't designed to be caterpillars. We were always meant to fly.

Let's look at each of the five paradigms and what it means to retain them in the workplace:

1. Teacher Knows Best

- Who makes all the decisions in your organization? Is it only the most senior people?
- How often are you consulted or asked openly for your perspective or considered opinion?

Teacher Knows Best is the paradigm we were taught when the prime purpose of the relationship between student and teacher was the transfer of knowledge and when the classic subjects we learned were factual, technical and not open to interpretation.

$2 + 2$ **always** equalled 4.

The hottest part of the Bunsen burner flame was *always* the top of the inner blue part.

I *always* went before E (except after C) and all that …

The rules of science and the core principles of many other subjects aren't up for grabs when we study them at school and we're not asked for our opinion on them at the time that we're taught them.

This is how you do this calculation. This is the principle or technique you need to remember.

Depending on the subject, many of the exams we sat tested our powers of recall and application, rather than asking for open-ended, opinion-based, all-options-considered possibilities to a problem or challenge with no defined solution.

Back then, Teacher *did* know best. Back when we couldn't dress ourselves properly or eat our sandwiches at lunchtime without getting jam all over our face. It was only as we got older and moved into more senior levels of learning, that our 'education' began to match more closely the ongoing growth, development and life-long learning of an adult experience. As adults, life's more open-ended.

It's as adults that we build our careers and seek to fulfil our potential, in a world of multiple answers with varying perspectives and solutions to the variety of challenges and opportunities that present themselves in any normal, working environment. And alongside getting dressed and showing up to work on time, we now have mortgage accounts and households to manage, domestic responsibilities and a social life to juggle, alongside navigating the rhythms and rigours of everyday life with friends and families and life's celebrations and challenges. We acquire competencies, have experiences and develop perspectives, many of which might have use or application in the day jobs we do.

No adult has a monopoly on experience. No one person owns all truth. This means *many* of us might have the answer, or could be part of the solution. A few people working together might collectively 'know best'. And any of us can be leaders given the right context. Few commercial scenarios exist where a single person knows best the way they did when we wore short trousers and took pencil cases to the schoolroom.

How can they? In large organizations, people in the 'more junior' parts of an operation are aware of things the senior people aren't privy to. They're closer to the action. They observe the organization from a hands-on, close-up perspective. They know things the teacher doesn't. And that includes some of the solutions to an organization's challenges.

Your boss can never be as close to the action as you are. But when boss becomes teacher and Teacher Knows Best, we create a bottle-neck, slow our response to address critical issues and close the door on valuable ideas and perspectives. And at the same time, organizations know there are great and well-needed ideas out there … but how to capture them?

Does your organization have an 'ideas' scheme? Does it have a suggestion box or a programme for gathering improvement ideas? Have you been to brainstorms, where you generated alternatives to working practices that would improve things for customers and workers, for shareholders, for everyone?

How well are they working? How many of the ideas have been implemented?

What happened to the ideas that filled all your flip charts?

Some suggestion schemes work effectively, but sadly, most don't. They fail to get long-term traction and executives sit in boardrooms scratching their heads as to why. Maybe School with Pay's running your particular show, even if the main players can't recognize it. When the underlying culture, leadership, decision-making and policy development of an organization is laced with a Teacher Knows Best paradigm, why would anyone put in effort to make a suggestion? If $2 + 2$ is **always** going to be 4, why waste time trying to improve it?

Teachers that always Know Best stand at the front of the class, scrawling on the chalk board. They ask us for the answers, but if our hands don't raise quickly enough, they put us out of our misery.

It's easier to dictate an answer than create space for people to discover it for themselves.

Teacher might Know Best. But not always.

When we start taking responsibility for our own opinions and doing our own **Thinking**, we begin to make our presence felt and leave the classroom behind us.

2. Do What You're Told

How would you describe the tone of voice of the organization you work for? What does it sound like and how does it talk to you?

Teachers establish their authority early in our schooling and largely for our protection, because at that stage they know a whole lot more than we do. The teacher and the construct of a 'lesson' bring a framework to education that would otherwise be left to chance. Fair enough. You only have to see toddlers running into a nursery to know they'll need a grown-up to run things properly. Doing What You're Told makes sense when you can't see the danger in running around with your coat over your head, or standing near a swing to take a closer look at the action, or when you wonder what happens when you let go of a spinning roundabout, or whether it's possible to swim with one armband (*been there, done all that*). Doing What You're Told when you're a potential danger to yourself and others makes sense.

Young children *should* do what they're told ... to start with. But at this early stage, the main purpose of doing what you're told is to establish a safe environment in which we can learn. Its roots are in *possibility*, not authority. Once that framework has served its useful purpose, this second paradigm falls away, as teachers and lecturers move from authority to facilitation and students move from 'learning the method' to more independent and thought-filled learning and self-discovery.

It seems to me that we've held on to too much of what went on in our elementary classrooms and that **Do What You're Told** has become a retained way of operating for many managers or executives; a trump card we overplay and which treats people like children. Whatever the boss says goes, so 'Just Do What You're Told' (with optional curse words added).

Do What You're Told is also what happens when the appropriate authority of any line manager becomes over-inflated and so their reports assume they can never be challenged, questioned or asked to debate an opinion. Teamwork, group-think and personal leadership don't survive when we all just do what we're told. When this paradigm becomes a habit and our default way of working, we leave our brains at the door and hand all our personal power and influence to the teachers we report to.

Do What You're Told came from the playground and should diminish as we grow and develop into maturity. Some organizations seem more focused on the power a particular position gives someone to exert authority, rather than focusing on the opportunities that authority creates to establish developmental environments which spark personal growth and enable discovery in people and teams.

> *You think the people of this country exist to provide you with position. I think your position exists to provide those people with freedom, and I go to ensure that they get it …*
> **William Wallace, Braveheart**

'Following the leader' because we can't lead ourselves as toddlers should eventually give way to individuals taking responsibility as adults in a business. **We should be doing good work,**

not avoiding a detention. This doesn't suggest resisting or rejecting an effective chain of command or deny the need for decision-making authority and protocols where necessary, but the problem with this way of thinking outside elementary education is that it emphasizes authority in a single individual, limiting the opportunities for collective challenge and an effective back-and-forth.

Blindly Doing What You're Told hands more power and influence to your boss than is necessary or useful in delivering peak performance. When you give power to another, you by definition make them power-**FULL** and yourself power-**LESS** and so you will feel even less able to challenge, question or effect change.

Since when did you hand another a gun, to shoot at your feet and make you dance?

There's already enough power at play in the command structures and operational frameworks we work in without you and I topping up the level of our own volition. When this happens, adult commercial relationships regress to resemble the school playground, falsely raising the barriers of authority to restrict performance, diminish collaboration and reduce the effectiveness of working relationships.

But let's just pause for a second. Maybe I hear a 'yes, but ...' with some of this.

Doing What You're Told clearly works in some commercial adult situations. I appreciate that it's valuable in the high-risk, life-and-death work of the emergency services, military and many aspects of healthcare. We wouldn't appreciate the fire service or a cardiac medical team debating and reviewing their next move by committee while smoke billows under the door of our bedroom or when we're having a bypass procedure. In these scenarios, an effective chain of command is essential and compliance is mandatory. But if we're honest, for most of us, the work we do isn't that clear cut. There isn't one single answer.

For the vast majority of people reading this book, outstanding performance and breakthrough innovation comes from the *sharing* of ideas, the consideration of alternatives and through teams of people working *together* to devise fresh strategies or develop breakthrough products. In these scenarios, blind compliance and subservience to Teacher does nothing except close down our talents and load responsibility onto the team leader. And whilst no leader is perfect, in School with Pay, the boss almost *has* to be, because they're now on their own when it comes to opinions in this particular team …

- **True leaders understand that they don't have to constantly be at the front of the class.**
- **True leaders don't need to remind their students who's in charge or who's running this lesson.**
- **True leaders set the tone and direction and then focus on getting the best out of everyone.**

When you remove Do What You're Told, leadership becomes a dynamic and collective discipline aligned around outcomes, rather than confined to a structure chart or hierarchical office. When you remove Do What You're Told as a workplace paradigm, people can leave school and take personal responsibility.

Think about where Do What You're Told might be present in your own organization or company:

- To what extent are you free to organize the work you do or the part of the business that you lead?
- How collaboratively do you make decisions in your operational teams and working groups?
- When do you (if you're a manager) switch to 'Tell' mode before giving your team a chance to develop their own thinking on an issue?

Do What You're Told. Always and without question.

But what if you began to innovate and started focusing on **Creativity**?

3. Don't Answer Back

What happens when your boss makes a statement or gives an opinion you or those around you disagree with?

Remember when we were told not to answer back when we were young children? I think we all were. And then all too quickly, we become adults and soon find ourselves telling our very own children the very same thing.

Don't Answer Back. Ever. It's very simple.

On the surface, this paradigm is again pretty reasonable in a well-mannered, respectful environment. At school, it's important for children to learn the parameters in relationships and to respect authority. We were told that our teachers knew best (which they did) and so, by extension, we shouldn't answer back when they were exerting their authority. We were there primarily to listen and our opinion, whilst interesting, was largely irrelevant if it didn't match what it said in the text book. Fair enough. But, as I've already described, school *prepared* us for the adult world but shouldn't define it.

Respecting others or being well-mannered are great working paradigms. In fact, I wish more people had them, particularly those I commute with every day. But in the workplace, I think we've twisted Don't Answer Back to suit our own needs. School with Pay, as ever, takes an innocent-on-the-surface paradigm and distorts it; adding hierarchy, authority and fear and preventing effective communication between adult working professionals.

Don't Answer Back removes natural and effective conversation and debate along with the validity and richness of differing opinions. This mindset results in interactions that are again contaminated by hierarchy and where 'junior' people fall silent as soon as Teacher has spoken. It's an unhelpful way of working.

Look out for the Don't Answer Back paradigm at work in your meetings, conversations or work-related discussions. You'll find it. Here's how it plays out in a meeting where one of the people present is the Teacher.

1. Agenda item, issue, challenge or discussion point raised. Conversation develops.
2. Group members offer opinions or perspectives back and forth with energy, until there's one that Teacher doesn't agree with.

3. Teacher voices their disagreement.
4. Brief awkward silence.
5. Discussion closed.

Don't Answer Back.

The worst example is where Teacher speaks first, creating an interaction that looks like this:

1. Agenda item, issue, challenge or discussion point raised.
2. Teacher gives their opinion.
3. Discussion closed.

Whatever you do, Don't Answer Back.

Don't Answer Back isn't about what's going on for the senior person or people in these interactions – it's about what's happening *with you and your* reactions. *You're* the one who's decided not to answer back, and despite all the reasons you'd try to explain to me, they could all be traced to some sort of *fear*. Corporate fear that stops us from answering back, asking questions or making valid challenges. School with Pay only works if there's fear in play somewhere.

When Don't Answer Back is present in our thinking, group and individual behaviour shifts people from making valid and appropriate contributions, to 'not answering back', for fear of being told off by Teacher. Look out for stilted and unnatural conversations in your organization, where offering a challenge is seen as 'insubordination' and those who do it regularly get pushed to the corners of the organization to think about what they've done.

This is not to defend rudeness, belligerence or someone who constantly opposes an agreed direction or team ethic. It's about great ideas that go unmentioned and negative behaviours that never get called out, or whispers in corridors rather than honest dialogue.

Why is it that in the adult workplace we're rarely truly candid with our bosses until something triggers us to spill our long-held-onto beans, sometimes causing explosions that are far more damaging than if our thoughts or perspectives had been expressed sooner or dealt with more quickly. Why is it that all the most robust conversations seem to happen in the movies and yet in the workplace, under the guise of 'professionalism', we reduce adults-sharpening-adults to a form of passive-aggressive, political backside-covering?

It could all be … so … much … easier. If we weren't still thinking like schoolchildren.

To what extent has Don't Answer Back found its way into your team or company?

- When are the times that you choose to avoid healthy and adult debate with someone in authority, or back down if your boss is the one who's disagreed with you?
- How comfortable are you personally with a debate? How do you react when you're challenged by people more junior than you (or, in fact, does it rarely seem to happen and what might *that* tell you)?

Don't Answer Back, because Teacher is scary.

49

Or **Believe** in your power and stop handing it over so freely.

4. Don't Copy

How well do people collaborate in your organization? What happens when you have a good idea and what do you do with it?

Is success open-sourced in your team ... or are people still competing, checking league tables every few days and reminding all around them who's Top Dog this week, month or moment?

Operating in silos. Protectionism. Lack of collaborative thought. Factions. Empire building. Position defending. Blame. Failed matrix management. Dysfunctional cross-functional working. Politics. Secrecy. Cliques. Distrust.

Doesn't sound good. But most of us have been there. Where do these working styles come from?

Operating in Silos = Bad.

Except in the classroom, when the focus was *our* work and silos were our only example.

Cross-functional Working = Good.

But don't talk in class please. And *never* in the exam hall. You can't even share a calculator.

In school it's copying. And we shouldn't do it.

At work it's collaboration. And we should. Except we never learnt *how*.

How can we expect to collaborate effectively when one of the dominant paradigms we were taught from our early years was to not copy, to do our own work and to cover our answers when the time came for a spelling test?

Don't Copy in the workplace means we hold onto our ideas, protect our perspectives and react badly when people want to develop them. We work happily in silos, aggressively defending territory and becoming divisive and critical of 'other' groups and teams in an organization, even though they might have a stake in our collective success. It's the adult equivalent of covering the test paper with your hand so that the annoying kid sitting next to you can't see your answers. Don't Copy at work means I cover all my answers and even if you're a colleague, if you're 'stuck', you're on your own. And then later, in another situation, if I'm stuck, *I'm* now the one isolated.

And the clock keeps ticking in the corner while everyone scribbles furiously on their answer sheets.

Time's up. Put your pens down please.

Some time ago, I spent a couple of years running a contact centre in the North West, which was divided into five different operational teams. Back then, a key aspect of running a contact centre was monitoring the 'calls abandoned' rate; the proportion of calls where the customer hung up or 'abandoned' the call before it had been directed to someone in one of the teams to answer. No customer likes hanging on the end of the phone waiting for it to be answered and the whole department was targeted to ensure that 95 percent of the people calling us got through and were quickly helped with whatever they needed. For our stake-holders, the abandon rate was *everything*.

I arrived as the new Operations Manager to turn around our service levels, which had suffered as a result of some unexpected staff changes. The calls abandoned rate was running well above 20 percent, meaning that more than 1 in 5 of the people who rang us eventually gave up. We had to change something.

My first team meetings were an eye-opener. The departmental metrics looked bad, but when I looked at the individual team statistics, they showed a marked variation in performance. The calls abandoned in two of the five teams were comfortably within service level on a consistent basis, whereas the three remaining teams were really struggling. We were using RAG (Red, Amber or Green) codes for each service measure and one team in par-ticular was deeply 'in red' across almost all their key metrics. In fact, their abandon rate suggested that more people gave up on their call than actually got through to eventually speak to someone.

I remember leaning back in my chair as I sat around a small table with my team managers as they reviewed the coloured summary sheet of our departmental performance. Two of the managers seemed super comfortable and confident. One looked like they'd prefer to be anywhere except sitting in this meeting and the remaining managers were trying to stay un-noticed.

Was I missing something here? How had this become a normal way of working for this team?

It didn't take long to understand that while two of my five-strong management team got on like a house on fire, they both had a problem with one of their team-mates. And the results were right there, screaming in front of us. This was Don't Copy at its worst. Forty percent of the team were flying, and yet covering their answers as though in an exam hall and were in fact keen to increase the gap with their less successful colleagues. And all the while, the manager of the team that was 'bottom' of the performance table was back in the form room, sitting with their arm raised, hoping that a teacher, their assistant or in fact *anyone* would help them.

How had this operations team let it come to this? What was the impact on our customers, who might be getting great service from one team and the opposite from another, while all of us were representing the same well-known, premium brand?

This team needed to understand that a high performing service centre isn't a spelling test. I asked for some changes to the way the numbers were presented each day, so that if one team was 'red', the *whole* team was 'red'. None of us would be seeing green any time soon unless these five managers found a different way of working together. It took a while and was far from perfect but in a few short weeks we recovered performance and maintained it through the time that team were together.

Collaboration is the future, with group success the preferred currency. Group-think is everything, and covering your work won't get you there. Adult life is real-time and global, crowd-sourced and crowd-funded; today's jobs are think-tanks, where ideas live in incubators ... and where a few lads chilling in a bedroom can get the whole world dancing when an idea goes viral.

Whilst there's clearly a difference between collaboration and stealing, Don't Copy seems strangely outdated in today's digital workplace. The days of covering your answers and being congratulated for getting there by yourself are over. It's all about *us* now. The age of open-source development, integrative design and collaborative outcomes demands that we lift our hands from our answers and to get used to sharing the thoughts we're having …

Is there anywhere, right now in your role, where you're covering your work up?

Are there people you'd benefit from collaborating with, but who you're secretly competing with, which stops you from picking up the phone? How's that working out for you?

Don't Copy. At school.

Connect and Collaborate. At work … if you know how to.

5. (Play Nicely and) Stay out of Trouble

Although on the surface this paradigm seems sound, I'm interested in its impact on the way we behave as individuals in organizations or teams. An over-emphasis on 'staying out of trouble' will lead some of us to keep our heads down, our noses clean and do whatever it takes not to rock the boat. Don't stand out, don't be noticeable and don't get labelled as a trouble-maker.

Stay Out of Trouble as a general rule is a good thing, obviously. But when you add Play Nicely and transfer it to the workplace, it begins to resemble Do What You're Told, and in a childish, schooling context it can again become about control.

Don't cause bother. Don't get in any trouble. Help Teacher's day go smoothly. Don't give Teacher any issues, because there are too many of you to deal with. Just ... play ... nicely. And make sure you stay out of trouble.

Nice. It's the word no-one wants to hear as an answer:

'How do I look tonight?' *Nice.*

'What do you think of the meal I just cooked?' *Nice.*

'What do you think of the colour of my new carpet?' *Nice.*

No-one wants *nice.* Nice means something's missing.

Playing Nicely and Staying Out of Trouble all the time reduces work to a vanilla, cookie-cutter, cartoon world where no-one stands out, we all go with the flow and everyone behaves themselves. Breakthrough performance or game-changing innovation rarely come from Staying Out of Trouble. How many history-making, sport-defining team performances have you seen where everyone played nicely and then skipped off into the sunset together?

Playing Nicely and Staying Out of Trouble means we suppress anything controversial, resulting in dysfunctional or poor quality behaviour going unchallenged, organizational issues remaining unresolved and development of a lack of integrity in professional relationships. Some of us have been taught from an early age not to be noticed or to stand out in a crowd.

Organizations with a Stay Out of Trouble paradigm become environments where fewer and fewer people seem to 'have a view'. What I mean by this, is that whilst people clearly *have* a view, they're not bold enough to express it. They play safe and they bury their thoughts and opinions, because speaking out around here is too risky. Opinions and perspectives that challenge the status quo and yet could also result in a breakthrough are 'shared in confidence' with safe supporters, but get moth-balled or shelved because the stakes are simply too high. Ideas get confined to history because the effort to engage in the process of landing them is just too great. Experienced people become chameleons, operating in whichever way will be best received, go down well with 'the bosses' or protect their current position, reputation and pension plan.

Where in your organization do the 'real meetings' happen and by 'real' I mean 'the-real-meetings-after-the-recent-meeting' meetings? 'Real' meetings are the sub-group, whispered corridor discussions and post-conversation conversations that should have happened *in* the meeting, if the invitees hadn't decided to Play Nicely (and Stay Out of Trouble). *Real* opinions, *real* objections, *real* root causes and *real* feedback only gets discussed freely among a sub-group or pairing, where the stakes for expressing true opinions are low enough for people to say what they've really been thinking or feeling. Real meetings are sometimes the only place where real business gets done.

The problem here is that the only way a real interaction can happen is if the work that's gone before has been *unreal*. Unreal conversations and meetings happen too regularly. The agenda is clear, the issues to discuss are well-known, except that when Teacher chairs the meeting, our Playing Nicely opens the door to unreality. We don't say what we really think, we fail to address the real issues, we 'bottle' the opportunity to engage with the elephant in the room and so waste an hour, two hours or longer in interactions of unreality. We played nicely and we stayed out of trouble. For now. But we didn't achieve a whole lot, did we?

Have you ever been in a meeting where someone has been asked a question, and where they've given an answer where their body language and non-verbal leakage have 'said' the exact opposite of the words that have come out of their mouth? They're trying to play nicely, right there, focused on staying out of trouble:

'I'm fiiiiine with it' (which clearly means I'm not)

'Yep, understood' (while desperately trying to stop their head from shaking)

'Leave it with me' (even though I have no idea what I'm going to do with it)

Or the nervous laugh (so I don't have to put words to my 'real' reaction)

Or worse still, silence (and with a smile that says the opposite)

Playing Nicely and Staying Out of Trouble works for a child learning how to respect other people's space, needs and sensibilities. No-one liked the school brat. But when you transfer the paradigm to the workplace and overlay it with authority, *always* playing nicely and *always* staying out of trouble blunts the cutting edge of fresh insight, kills boldness and stifles innovation, while every organization on the planet searches hard for all three.

The superstars in your company won't always play nicely. The true innovators might create a little trouble. They might even be high-maintenance. But commercially they could just be your game-changers and are people to attract, retain, develop and leverage. Being disruptive and causing a little trouble might help you out-perform your competition and I'm convinced many performances would improve if a few great people would drop the pseudo-politeness and call out what's needed. We're all busy people.

No-one needs to be rude. But I do wish we were a lot less polite.

- Where might you be Playing too Nicely?
- Where might Trouble be *exactly* what you should be getting into right now, if only you were bold enough?

(Play Nicely and) Stay out of Trouble.

Except what would your work and performance look like if you could believe **All is Well**?

* * *

Five simple paradigms, which might have worked in school. But we were never supposed to take them beyond the school gates.

Except some of us did return. Some of us found ourselves in jobs that caused us to return to familiar ways of thinking.

We've already seen that after all the excitement and promise, many of us arrived in the workplace, only to turn around and walk right back through the school gates of our own thinking and performance. Many of us are school-leavers who never really left.

School with Pay is about our Thinking and Attention as individuals.

And where our Attention is, is where we'll all Go.

Teacher Knows Best

*But what would it be like if we all started **Thinking**?*

Do What You're Told

*Except isn't adult life all about **Creating**?*

Don't Answer Back

*But would we know how to if only we **Believed** in ourselves?*

Don't Copy

*Except what do you do when workplace **Connections** are your currency?*

(Play Nicely and) Stay out of Trouble

*But what if we were less fearful and did our jobs as though **All was Well**?*

THE GAMES WE PLAY(ED)

School has structure. Work has structure. But as we've seen, a School with Pay mindset and its five paradigms in a business will hold us all back and keep us in uniforms; as individuals, as teams and always as organizations.

School with Pay takes the thinking that birthed registers and year groups, subject streaming and the staff room and transfers it to an enterprise or business, creating scenarios that reveal we're still queuing for assembly or wearing elasticated ties. Think back to the conventions and protocols that underpinned your own school community. If this kind of dynamic presents itself in your commercial environment, how might it impact the working atmosphere, or emerge now and then in your protocols and processes? What would the impact be on your performance and effectiveness and the overall extent to which you Showed Up?

Put your hands up, quietly, if you think know the answer ...

Stand Up for Teacher – how everything changes once the boss is about

Conversations and laughter, action and movement. A classroom of kids gathering for morning registration is perfect youthful chaos; the sharing of experiences, the obsessions of the moment and the details of the day that here, right now, are critically important. It's buzzing. It's moving.

And then the teacher strolls through the doorway. The noise subsides and uncomfortable chairs scrape and slide back in a single united action.

We were taught to stand when teacher arrived in the classroom.

Have you noticed the way people behave around 'the bosses' in organizations – the way a meeting tone can change when a senior person enters the room or how the body language of a group alters when someone in authority walks across the office?

Some of us still Stand Up for Teacher.

How does your own behaviour change when your line manager's with you? Are you respectful of their position and yet maintain your poise and personal presence, or do you react internally as though they're walking your corridor, checking for dust on the cabinets of your language and performance?

Consider how you react when you're in discussion with colleagues and an executive appears on the scene, or the vibe of your interactions and meetings when the team leader is either present or absent. Is there a difference? If you're honest, does your heart rate speed up just a little whenever they're around? Are you slightly more aware of how you express your opinions, the words you choose and the level of honesty with which you express them? Do you alter your behaviour and begin to present an ever-so-slightly-adjusted version of yourself?

Maybe you're standing, waiting for permission to sit.

Incidentally, this dynamic also happens in reverse, for leaders who seem to demand a salute from their direct reports whenever they arrive on the scene. Do you notice, or perhaps secretly enjoy it, when the room around you falls silent on your arrival?

Don't diminish your impact and contribution by leaping to attention when a 'boss' appears on the horizon. Giving away that much power doesn't help anybody and certainly not the people leading you. And if you're a manager, quit playing Teacher as you navigate your working week – you might just miss your team giggling as they take their seats.

- When you're around 'more senior' people, how authentic is your behaviour?
- How 'real' are you and would your friends and family recognize you?

Registration – what's really going on in your meetings

Our school classrooms were organized in long rows and we kept our bags on top of our desks at registration. In part, this was to make a quick getaway to whichever lesson was first period that day. It also worked well as a pillow to catch up on the sleep we should have had the night before, but more often than not, it was to hide what we were really doing.

I observe Registration behaviours in team meetings, offsites and engagement sessions with almost every client I work with. Gone are the bags and the giggling (maybe), but the underlying behaviours and instincts ring as true as ever. What makes the difference between a meeting where everyone is engaged and switched on and other sessions we've been in, where a few of the attendees are staring out of the window, only to jump to attention when their name is called?

The problem with registration is that it wasn't created for *us*. It wasn't structured for *our* benefit. Registration was for the machine and to ensure that the administrative requirements of the school would be met, delivering good governance and adequate care for the schoolchildren in its care. It was a roll call – who was there, who wasn't and a chance for the key messages of the day to be communicated and for daily admin to be taken care of. We didn't have ownership or a stake in any of it. So we played behind our bags or stared out of the window.

How many team meetings, huddles or communication sessions took place in your company this morning that followed this model? How many 'meetings' were simply a broadcast of instructions rather than creating a platform for everyone in the team to make a contribution in the day ahead of them?

It's time to reinvent many of our meetings and gatherings. Some of us need to change the way we engage with our teams, because right now, we're fooling ourselves with an approach that simply walks us and our teams back into the classroom. True engagement can be judged from the response you provoke in people, not what you think you communicated to them. True 'engagement' leaves each person *feeling* that word and gives everyone a personalized version of how they fit, in the goal that's bigger than all of us.

And when that happens, we take our bags off the desk, we shift our eyes forward and get ready to make something happen.

- How 'engaging' are the meetings that you have in your diary, or are lying there waiting in the few days ahead of you?
- What would it take for every person attending them to fully present and not distracted?
- Is the purpose of your meetings clear and do you know their outcome?
- What would be different, or might everything be the same, even if you cancelled them?

Stay Out of the Staff Room – asking for help and the curse of a closed door

We were scared of visiting the staff room. It was at the end of a dark corridor and behind a big green door with no window. You had to knock and wait for someone to answer. We rarely got a huge smile or a rapturous welcome. 'Mmm?' or 'Yes, what is it?' was the stock response from a teacher munching a biscuit, with a frown accompanying the question; a reminder that this wasn't your space and that you weren't particularly welcome.

Asking for help at work can feel like heading back to visit the Staff Room. Your answer is behind a big door that's closed, from people who'd rather not be interrupted. It means some of us stay silent, struggling in our confusion. Yet for most of us, our work is full of questions and riddled with enquiries; work is a team pursuit and yet our mindset leaves us behaving like it's the opposite.

When there's too much authority in play in our workplaces, we become reluctant to ask for help, admit confusion or ask for clarification for fear it will be received as weakness or that stakeholders will think less of us. The Staff Room creates a mentality where we're under constant review, and some defend this position as 'the reality of business' or 'life in the real world'. What we fail to recognize is that by subscribing to this, we heap pressure on ourselves to hold all the answers, viewing a question repeated as a mark of poor performance that Teacher will make a note of on our summer report cards.

School with Pay offices have staff rooms. Experienced people making valuable commercial contributions are reduced to schoolboys and schoolgirls when summoned to see the boss or interact with executives. Increased heartbeats. Dry mouths. Sweaty palms. And laughter in the right places at any of the jokes they make.

- Where do you need support right now, or would benefit from a hint or 'top tip' from an expert?
- What's your reaction to asking for help and is it getting in the way of gaining a solution?
- Is there a question you have or issue you need help with, which you've buried under the carpet in case it might make you 'look bad'? How's that approach working out for you?

Show and Tell – make sure you notice me

We'd arrive at school clutching our bag and excited about its contents. Inside was our item, the thing we were going to talk about and we'd all get a turn eventually. Not surprisingly, few of us remembered items brought in by others. Show and Tell was *our* message, it was *our* object and this would be *our* story.

School with Pay creates the same workplace dynamic – Corporate Show and Tell.

Corporate Show and Tell is what happens when we move from contribution to competition and work becomes a race to see who can shout loud enough. You've probably seen Corporate Show and Tell in action. It's in the person who dominates a meeting with their own stories, arguments and perspectives. We recognize it in an occasional team member who constantly feels the need to highlight their own performance and remind us of what they (I) did, in case any of us forgot or overlooked their achievements.

Show and Tell is often found in business performance meetings, where 'the numbers' are reviewed, along with progress against an operating plan. Whether face to face or by webinar/conference call, Corporate Show and Tell reveals those I call the Question Monitors; people who ask tricky questions, not because they're hugely valid or serve a useful purpose, but in order to make themselves look good and in turn deflect the teacher's attention. Their questions are also designed to wrong-foot the people they've addressed them to and remind all of us who's got the most impressive Show and Tell item round here.

When teams play Show and Tell, no-one's actually listening. Individuals wait patiently, staring out of the window, or checking their email, until their moment comes because *their* item's the one we were all *really* waiting for. I was working with a couple of senior teams recently where Corporate Show and Tell was rampant. Performance review meetings took place on a weekly basis, chaired by the CEO but with an ever-increasing entourage of subject matter experts, external consultants and interested parties. The relevant business owners would file in or dial in, to review the results for their particular area. One executive described it as 'walking to the witness stand' every Monday.

Just think about this metaphor for a moment. An **experienced executive**, with organizational responsibility for hundreds of people, working as hard as they could in a role they'd been selected for, walking to 'the stand' every week, a witness for the prosecution.

Surely we can do better than a courtroom metaphor to describe the way we manage performance? What's happened to our personal power and presence when we engage in these scenarios?

Corporate Show and Tell is a game without winners.

- Where do you drift into Corporate Show and Tell in meetings when you feel 'you have to make a contribution'? Is that really working and are you showing the very best of yourself?
- How do you react to the Question Monitors; do you jump to find an answer or call them out on their game-playing?

- When do you choose to stay silent and let others take the limelight (and if this sentence reads like nonsense, what might *that* be telling you)?

*In June 2013 in Essex, UK, a nine-year-old pupil took an artillery shell to Show and Tell, alerting the police and scrambling an army bomb disposal team. That's **real** Show and Tell.*

The Red Pen – having your decisions marked

We handed it in and it was returned a few days later; peppered in the margins with the bright red pen of Teacher's comments and corrections, with maybe a final statement at the bottom. We didn't realize our homework would still be marked twenty years later, when we'd grown into adults and taken on responsibilities.

The Red Pen is what happens when effective governance is distorted by School with Pay thinking and means multiple layers of sign-off are required before decisions can be ratified. And it just might be getting worse out there. From what I can see, more and more managers have ever more senior people 'checking their work' before they can finalize their decisions, particularly when there's a cheque to be written. As ever, this is a subtle and on-the-surface reasonable distortion of a sensible principle. Financial and organizational decisions clearly need a process of effective approval and control, but has it got out of control in your workplace?

I've worked for two different companies when, following a spending review, the Finance Director announced cost-saving measures. Corporate travel would now need board level approval in advance and prior to bookings being made by individuals. Its introduction created carnage in the field unseen by 'the Centre' and if anyone based there had taken time to review the additional administration and time costs that had been *added* to the organization as a result of this policy, they'd likely have found a figure on their spreadsheet greater than the savings they'd projected.

Sadly, no-one did, but our sense of it hung in the air, its uneasy stench sticking in our throats. This policy likely meant a net **cost** to this business, before accounting for the negative impact it was having on experienced individuals and managers, whose daily decisions might receive a Red Pen-mark against them. This wasn't about money. It was about **control**. And it came directly from a School with Pay mindset – the underlying belief that competent people can't *really* be so, or that decisions will be wrong unless someone else checks them.

Teacher Knows Best. But it might just cost us more.

There's a difference between Teacher's Red Pen and an effective and appropriate chain of command. I'm also convinced that most people know the difference between the two without needing to be checked or reminded. When they're engaged in the commercial objectives and outcomes of a business, most professionals are more than equipped for effective decision-making and good stewarding of company resources. But how many of our systems, processes and approval protocols reflect this belief? Some of them seemed designed as though, given the chance and if no-one was looking, there'd be anarchy in the classroom and tears before bedtime.

The opposite of control isn't freedom, it's **trust**. When trusted, most of us respond in kind; working harder, committing more and bringing more to the party and improving the environment for everyone in the process. Trust doesn't feel the need to mark people's homework, and when people are trusted, better work might get done. And if you don't believe that, might *you* resemble a Teacher?

Check your pens people. The colour you're using might just surprise you.

- How often does your work get marked in the office? And if and when that sort of thing happens, how do you react?
- Do you revert to being a student or do you take the time to re-negotiate the terms of this adult working relationship, clarifying the parameters and establishing trust rather than resentment?
- Where are you marking your colleagues work, rather than trusting them to get on with it? What do you need that you haven't yet received and which prompted you to bring the Red Pen out (e.g. reassurance, an update, a sense of their ownership or a vibe they're all over it?) How about taking a moment to discuss it in full with them and improve their overall experience of working with you?

Forgetting Your Homework – what happens when we make a mistake

What's the reaction when mistakes happen in your workplace? What happens internally when you forget to do what you prom-ised, when you have no idea what the answer is, or when you slowly realize that you've totally misunderstood the brief you were given? What about if you just got it plain wrong, cocked-up or made a mistake?

In School with Pay, everyone makes mistakes. As long as it's not *you* and as long as it's not *here*.

Except high performing teams operate with a mindset that's *fearless* (more on that later). High performing teams are populated by high performing adults ... and some of them forget to do their homework. They also deliver work of high quality and occasionally produce a masterpiece. The stories we quote of companies and individuals that sparked true innovation, extreme creativity and ground-breaking breakthroughs are often riddled with tales of 'failure', mistakes and set-backs that went un-noticed along the way.

Even geniuses forget their homework.

It was a focus on the big picture of what they were creating and who they were becoming that made all the difference – it was what happened *next* and what they learnt from the experiences that was critical, not the fear of receiving a black mark from Teacher. If our working environments lack the open and supportive capacity for people to get things wrong and make mistakes, we'll *all* miss incredible opportunities for growth, development and original thinking.

For most of us, our mistakes are rarely critical in the long term and they nearly always deliver a better resolution when acknowledged more openly and used in support of our development. Mistakes provide valuable feedback that reveals key areas for improvement – and they'll never be found if we hide them from the Teacher. We have to move 'making mistakes' from the classroom to the *research lab* and see them as a fundamental part of life, growth, creativity and innovation. In a research lab, every failure is one step closer to a possible breakthrough.

- How do you react when you make an error while you're working? Do you head back to school? What are your instinctive responses and what might they be telling you?
- How do you react when others get things wrong? What environment have you created for the people who make mistakes around you?

Sick Notes at Games Lessons – the death of creativity

I loved sports at every stage of my school life. I tried out for most teams and Games (physical education) was the first thing I looked for in each year's lesson timetable. Watching, practising and competing at sports was (and still is) me at my happiest. I never understood the kids who brought sick notes to games lessons or who hated the banter of a changing room and the pursuit of a hard-fought victory.

Sick note? Me? Never.

But what I didn't get was Music. Or Art. Or Drama.

I appreciated the fact that others excelled at them, I enjoyed their productions and the performances of experts, but the practice of doing it myself just didn't work for me ... or anyone else that heard me trying to master some chime bars on my own (remember those?) or render a drawing with charcoals that kept breaking. Give me a ball, 'cause I'm wasted in the art-room.

Or am I? Could it be that I *am* a secret artist or a budding performer, but that those skills have just never been developed?

Sir Ken Robinson is a leading voice in educational reform and creativity who describes traditional education as 'dislocating people from their natural talents'. He describes an unspoken hierarchy in education that prioritizes Mathematics, Languages and the Humanities and relegates subjects like Art, Music, Drama and Dance. According to Robinson, as our children get older, we educate them 'progressively from the waist up, focusing on their heads ... and slightly to one side' (the left).[1]

Would you benefit from greater level of creativity in your business?

Would improved 'presence', public speaking abilities and the freedom and confidence of your leaders to get loose and deliver an occasional virtuoso performance generate greater engagement and energy in the teams they serve? Could you do with some more artists among your teams of mathematicians? And if so, does your organization have the cultural bandwidth to accommodate difference; people with different skills, different needs and different styles and ways of working?

I rejected Music in the same way others rejected the Sports Hall. But our rejections came from limited information and with

---

[1] *How Schools Kill Creativity*, TED 2006.

next-to-no experience, largely based on the resources our particular school had available. Mine only had one decent drum kit. And it didn't offer archery. Pottery was led by a supply teacher and there was no river for us to row in. So I never learned how to do any of them.

Your business needs artists. It's crying out for performers.

Maybe you need to invest in a dance studio.

- Where are the sick notes being written in *your* organization?
- Where are people 'checking out' because your 'curriculum' is too narrow, too specialized or too scientific?
- Why are the so-called 'creative types' leaving your companies, because it's all about the numbers, or the banter of the changing room?

Parents' Evening – the monthly one-to-one

A brief five minutes with every teacher. A register filled with multi-coloured numbers, scrawled in rows alongside an alphabetized list of names. And chairs so small that adult legs nearly grazed their own chins.

Parents' Evening isn't a reciprocal conversation. The teacher offers facts, a few brief perspectives and maybe a couple of stories to underline the points they want to make and normally the parents walk away without questioning (because, of course, Teachers are right about *everything*). A good teacher might engage a little more deeply, but Parents' Evening is largely a series of one-way interactions; single perspectives lacking effective discussion. And even as parents, we still obey the five paradigms.

One-to-ones and performance reviews in School with Pay organizations mirror Parents' Evening. You sit quietly and patiently listen as your boss reads their verdict on how you've been doing; their one-way description of your performance for the period. You nod and suppress any instinct for frowning. At the end they ask if you have any questions, but of course you don't have questions – you're playing student and so Teacher Knows Best.

I recently met a manager who was eight months into a 'development secondment' – their chance to earn their stripes in a bigger and broader role. I asked how they were doing and they said they *simply didn't know*. As we talked I discovered they'd had *no* one-to-ones, had *no* agreed outcomes and so no target from which to assess their secondment. You can imagine the impact it was having on them and yet they'd done *nothing* to challenge it, because 'it was just how things happen round here' … and, of course, Teacher Knows Best. This secondment was specifically for their development, and yet 'development' was the one thing that specifically wasn't happening.

One-to-ones are conversations, not podcasts; they're enquiries, not news bulletins. We don't schedule 'one-to-ones' with our partners or our family. Real life is about *interaction*, it's about *exchanges* and *relationships*. If we manage performance through purposeful relationships, we don't need Parents' Evening.

Don't settle for conversations that are lifted from the form room. Only one person does any talking and the chairs are too small.

- How well are *you* doing in your job right now?
- How well are any people who work *for* you doing in their jobs right now?
- Do you and they both *know*, across both of these scenarios, with no shadow of doubt and with absolute confidence? What if I asked them and they emailed their answer to us?
- What do your answers to the above questions tell you about the sorts of conversations you've recently been having?

The School Report – performance management processes and protocols

As if it wasn't scary enough already, we had to write our own names on the brown envelope. We knew that eventually, they'd be opened and filled with a report card with our name on it. At my school, our reports were long and thin and resembled legal documents. We assumed they'd contain something bad. And if that wasn't enough, we had to take them home without opening them, then nervously wait while one or both of our parents read through them. It was the mental equivalent of forming a fist, before having to punch yourself in the face. Then we waited ... for the eyes to lift up from the report card they were holding ... for the pages to stop turning and for the awkward silence to be broken, when we'd finally learn what our immediate-term fate would be.

Performance management can be wonderful. It has the potential to be transformational, to maximize our potential and develop our thinking and take our performance to a level we would never have reached on our own. Except when it's School with Pay, when it's just another report card in another brown envelope.

Is true performance management *alive* in your workplace? Is it vibrant, breathing, colourful and engaging, as your organization hurtles towards goals that are compelling for *everyone*, where everyone's contribution is explicit and celebrated and where all our performances matter, because our mission is too important?

It could be. It *should* be.

The reality is, too many of us haven't even got a plan in place. Too many of the people I work with are unable to describe coherent or engaging personal objectives. A few are unable to remember them. We complete annualized, standardized, sanitized performance templates and meet the corporate timelines, but some of us are simply going through the motions. Idealized intention rather than actualized delivery. The paperwork gets stored in deep-buried folders or in drawers that never open. Then at half-year or maybe annually, we write our name on a small brown envelope and follow a process that we've seen somewhere before, when we had scabs on our knees and were waiting for a verdict.

- How inspired are you by the performance management you experience in your own organization?
- How hungry are you for a review with your boss, in the way an elite athlete watches tapes of recent performances to see where they can be just a little ... bit ... better?
- What might be the improvements, or 'updates' that are available to you?

Team Sheets and Hall Monitors – HR admin and 'people' processes

You'd hear the whispering long before you reached the notice-board. The teacher would wander down the corridor, ignoring the speculative questions and steering his way through the crowd of eager pupils. He'd finally break through the crowd and silently pin up the team sheet before stepping away quickly, as we pushed and shoved to see where our name was.

In junior school football, the best I could hope for was to be named as a sub. And I didn't always get that. I eventually improved but junior school football team selection was torture. For a while back there, I gave all my power to a team sheet I'd never make it onto. Ever felt like this?

Long before we ever read a sports teacher's team sheet, we were schooled in its principles in the informal playground games where teams were selected. The two strongest players in whichever game was being played were chosen as captains and then went through the rest of us, picking players in turn that they wanted on their side. I loved being captain, because it guaranteed you wouldn't get picked last.

No-one wants to be the one who's picked last in the playground. But it happened, at some point, to most of us as school kids. And yet of course, if our business is like School with Pay, every re-structure, minor re-organization or desk move take us all back to the playground, lined up against a wall, with unknown external influences determining our destiny. Insecure maybe, but then that's what the team sheet does to us. **Insecurity and Fear are School with Pay at its worst.**

Organizations expand and contract constantly, changing shape, splitting, combining, consolidating and dividing; a constant process of regeneration and reform. Organizational Design is a specialist discipline all of its own and the processes of formal consultation and implementation of large-scale change can take months or occasionally years to deliver. Alongside this, effective talent management and succession planning is the Holy Grail for many organizations.

Problem is, too many of us are giving power to the Team Sheet; concerned with whether we're 'in', rather than making our contribution; more obsessed with whether the captains like us, than in boldly fulfilling our individual potential. Few HR professionals seem to evolve beyond hall monitors with clipboards, focused more on administration than the outcomes the role was designed for. Few teams thrive when there are hall monitors round the corner. **School with Pay will always hold us back.**

If you're all about the team sheet, you'll twist yourself into whatever shape you think is necessary in order to fit in, regardless of whether it's a shape that suits you or not. It's a zero-sum game. You're not being yourself and we're not getting your true performance.

Stop checking the Team Sheet. Play Your Own Game.

- When did you work with your greatest level of confidence, where you never doubted your ability or questioned your contribution? What were the conditions, the environment and the circumstances?

- How might you re-create those in the work you do and the relationships you have with the people who are working with you?

Short Skirts and Skinny Ties – conforming to corporate 'rules'

School kids always bend the uniform rules. Whether it's lads turning their ties round to wear them on the skinny side, or girls rolling their skirts up to wear them as short as possible, most of our teachers spent a chunk of their time monitoring our uniform and policing for banned earring types. When I was a teenager, white socks were cool and we loved them. Honestly. But we couldn't wear them with everything. We weren't supposed to wear them to school. White socks didn't comply with the uniform. And I know they didn't comply, because one day I forgot about it …

The whole of my first day at secondary high school was carnage. Hundreds of new kids looking various shades of lost (particularly in the new blazers that were clearly two sizes too big for them), a handful of children in the corners crying softly and a few older teachers already counting the days until Autumn half-term. Central to the circus was Assembly – the annual gathering for every pupil and staff member, to hear the Principal set the scene and describe what was ahead for this academic year. We all filed in in an unfamiliar new year group; the confident seniors at the back and us nervous new kids at the front.

At the front. The very front. Front … and middle and opposite the Headmaster. Right under his nose.

And as I dropped to the floor to sit cross-legged on this, my first day in my new school and in front of the Headmaster, my bright white socks blinked loudly at everyone. The original schoolboy error. I quickly scanned along the rest of my line, desperately hoping someone else had made the same mistake among all the other newly pressed trousers and not-yet-scuffed school shoes. Nothing. Black or grey socks everywhere. I was on my own. With people I didn't know, among new friends I hadn't yet met, but who here, right now thought I was trying to be 'different'. And some teachers seemed to be frowning. It was a disaster.

Of course, first impressions *do* count and from my years in retail I appreciate full well the value of a well-executed corporate uniform and the critical need for immaculate standards on a sales floor. But School with Pay isn't about physical presentation or the importance of a professional image. It's about the way those standards are communicated and executed in large-scale operations and what, in turn, they often spark in our behaviour.

In one organization I worked at, a new CEO was appointed and undertook the usual full-business review and fact-finding exercise. He'd arrived with a strong track record and was personable and passionate – we were excited to hear more of his vision and the places he'd take us during the tenure of his leadership. You can imagine our disappointment when his first formal communication to his head office team centred on dress-code and office-wear standards, along with examples in case of uncertainty.

While he might have had a point and I respected his desire for standards, you can guess what our corridor conversations became focused on and the banter-filled 'uniform' auditing that now happened in every meeting. This was the *only* message he'd landed from our first experience of his leadership, which was lost in a mix of our ridicule and outrage. We'd been looking for far more direction. A poorly-timed and badly phrased 'engagement' saw us wandering back through the school gates of our own reactions and now finding new ways to be rebellious. When two years down the line this particular executive was still struggling to land his weekly blog and brief the division effectively, it was clear his updates were still received as though 'sent from The Principal'; a parental message to a workforce reacting like teenagers.

It's good to focus on personal presentation standards. But don't treat people like they're children in a classroom. Show each person working with you why having a standard is important and how it contributes to the success of your organization or venture.

Don't ban white socks just because they're not your personal preference. People like me forget.

- Are you clear on the brand standards of the organization you work for? What's the 'promise' of your company and how does it impact the way you present yourself?
- To what extent are you 'hall monitor', checking uniform for tradition, rather than as an extension of company brand values?
- How are you building pride and passion throughout the organization, not simply via a dress-code policy?

Running in the Corridors – corporate 'fun' and teambuilding exercises

Maybe it was the shiny floors that were so inviting. Or the way our speeding footsteps echoed off the hallway walls. Or perhaps all the small windows created the effect we were running faster than was possible. I don't know – but what I do know is that an empty corridor is perfect for running down when you're a kid. Even when you're not late for anything.

Running in the corridors at school was, of course, off limits. But that didn't mean it wasn't fun and the one thing our legs wanted to do when no-one was looking. The places we work are the same. **Every company has its own corridors that none of us are supposed to run down, even ones with amazing office buildings designed without any.** Corporate corridors are the established protocols and conventions that develop over time and that we're all expected to walk down in an orderly, robotic fashion; institutional walkways that keep everything flowing smoothly and ensure there are no accidents when the lesson bell goes. And just in case, and as we know, there are hall monitors somewhere, to make sure we all comply safely.

No Jumping, No Bombing and never any Heavy Petting ...

Some organizations have lost the ability to play. To laugh. To giggle uncontrollably at the most inappropriate moments and try things that serve no greater purpose other than looking like they could be enormous fun. Corridors were meant to be run down, we were born for play and laughter and many of our greatest ideas as a human race were stumbled across by accident and weren't discovered by following convention or by walking at a safe pace.

This isn't about anarchy; it isn't a call to remove useful boundaries or supporting structures, but it *is* a call for more freedom in our workplaces. It *is* a call to dismantle the corridors, to restore personality and colour to the way we work and to give laughter its rightful place in our day-to-day experiences. And it *is* a request to let people at least break into a jog in some corridors, because it's much more fun getting to a lesson that way ...

Our goal should be to create open and accepting teams and working environments, filled with enough authentic connections for genuine interest, affection and understanding between members to develop. When this happens, the very act of us gathering together generates an energy and fun all of its own, regardless of what we're doing, where we find ourselves and what's 'organized'. A few of the times when we've had the most fun were pre-planned and organized, but a whole load of our most memorable life experiences were events that just happened, where no-one took charge and where spontaneity drove what developed. It was probably because they *weren't* being organized for fun on those occasions, but because we'd just found a way to enjoy being together.

If you can't have 'fun' in the course of the work you do, it's unlikely to happen just because it's sign-posted, or when Teacher decides to organize an awayday for everyone.

- When's the last time you cried with laughter or let out your ultimate belly-laugh during a board meeting?
- When's the last time you wished a meeting wouldn't finish, because you were having such a great time?
- How many times last week did you figuratively run down the corridors of your organization, slide in the assembly hall with just your socks on, or hook your

coat-hood over your head and run in circles making airplanes?

Game(s) Over?

So, as we've seen, at school we all played games. Problem is, **some of us are still playing them.** Check out again the list of ways in which our outdated ways of thinking can create zero-sum games that we thought we'd grown out of:

Standing up for Teacher
Attending Registration
Fear of the Staff Room
Corporate Show and Tell
The Red Pen
Forgetting Your Homework
Sick Notes at Games Lessons
Parents' Evening
School Reports
Team Sheets and Hall Monitors
Short Skirts and Skinny Ties
Running in the Corridors

Five simple paradigms. Five ways of thinking. Five ways of operating which became ingrained in the ways we work and behave and that many of us ended up believing are still true. And the result of these paradigms taking hold is creating carnage; birthing restrictive operational structures, closing company cultures and releasing dysfunctional behaviours for thousands if not millions of us ... even though none of this is working for us. And if they're not working for us, they *definitely* won't be working for the customers of our organizations if they're operating under their spell.

As we've seen across a range of scenarios, the five School with Pay paradigms can be powerful and pervasive and, for some of us, have become old friends.

But think back to the Iceberg Dynamic.

Companies, teams and individuals with this mindset allow the waters of their oceans to rage wild and unmanaged, sweeping away the potential of entire groups of people and causing long-term commercial damage that can't always be recovered.

School with Pay slows us down, reduces innovation and collaboration and drains the colour from what should be a vibrant, creative, living, breathing working life and environment for us all.

I love work. I *love* it. And I *hate* School with Pay and all that it manifests.

If we can recognize and challenge the patterns of our own thinking and those of our businesses, there's a good chance we'll find a way to throw off our cocoons and finally leave school for good.

Leaving School means we're ready. It means it's time to start Showing Up.

SHOWING UP –
THE GATES ARE OPEN

The models of our early education mirror a production line, organizing students by date of birth and in pre-arranged subjects according to centralized standards and with operating paradigms that we've seen drive conformity, compliance and standardization.

Works if you're making engines.

Or door handles.

Or windows.

But not **people**.

The Power Exchange

The paradigms that underpinned the worlds in which we were educated as young children should fall away as we move into maturity and begin to take our place in the world. We're not supposed to think in the ways we did at school when we're working in a commercial environment and interacting with other adults. And if we do, it's likely that we're handing over personal control, authority, choice and self-expression to the Teacher, who'll take the lesson from this point forward.

School with Pay creates a wholly unhelpful and unnatural power exchange.

Think about it for a moment.

The five paradigms we were taught at school rightfully and understandably handed power in that context from the student to the teacher. Each of the five contains an underlying presupposition that an 'other' is in charge and that we are therefore subservient to them. And as we've already seen, carrying the reasonable constructs of an elementary educational environment into adulthood can be bad news for all of us.

The only way people in authority or with structural power can be positioned as 'teachers' is if you and I make them so, through the ways we think, behave, react and interact when we're around them. School with Pay can only exist in our thinking if there's a transfer of power from ourselves to another. We create these conditions all for ourselves and then suffer unnecessarily because of them.

And remember: *they* didn't do this, *you* and *I* did individually; and if you're operating with a distorted working dynamic as a result of your thinking and personal choices, there can always be alternatives and freshly updated ways of thinking.

Your boss isn't the Teacher naturally. They're just a boss. They have governmental authority and responsibility to set the direction of the work you do, but no individual can have power over another unless an exchange has taken place, from one person to another. For your manager to have become your teacher, you and your colleagues have to endow them with that power by adopting the five paradigms and giving them life in your particular workplace. As mentioned previously, giving power to another person by definition makes them more power*ful* and you more power*less*. And when you allow that exchange to happen, School with Pay begins to grow and can become the default mode of operating for your team, division or across the entire business.

School with Pay doesn't just happen, and it's not something done to us … it exists from the ways in which we're thinking. The people around you, whether your colleagues, bosses, stakeholders or customers, only have power if you allow them to. It is possible to be entirely conscious of another's authority, respectful of their position and aware of their influence without becoming the child to their adult and making yourself power*less* in the process. We'll see when we look at five *new* paradigms that it's possible to be in the presence of significant power and authority whilst retaining your own and still Showing Up in all of your fullness.

So how do we leave School with Pay?

The previous chapter helped us step back from what might have become embedded and habitual workplace behaviours to notice where the five old paradigms are present in our thinking and through the organizations we're part of.

Sometimes distance is all you need to gain perspective.

Once we see School with Pay for what it is, we have a new option. We can decide to leave.

Stop It

MADtv was a comedy sketch show that ran on Fox's Comedy Central channel between 1995 and 2008. One superb sketch featured the legendary comedian, Bob Newhart, playing a therapist offering support to Mo Collins, who played the patient. After listening as his patient described the debilitating problem she wished to discuss, he offered two words that he wanted her to 'listen to very carefully, before taking them out of the office with her and incorporating into her life'.

After the patient had excitedly reached for a notepad to write down what she expected would be simple yet life-changing advice from an expert, he simply leant across the table and shouted '**STOP IT!!**' in her shocked, unexpectant face. As the session continued and she described her condition in ever more detail, his advice as the therapist remained ever the same: **STOP IT!!**

'Stop It' has been viewed over a million times on YouTube.[1] It's a great sketch and not just because it's funny. It's great because it's exactly the type of 'therapy' some of us need in order to Leave School.

If School with Pay isn't working for you, your colleagues or your organization, **Stop It**.

Stop thinking that way. Stop working according to the five paradigms.

Do something different. Think something different. Be something different.

---

[1] Check out Stop It at www.youtube.com/watch?v=Ow0lr63y4Mw.

Make a decision to stop behaving like a student or to stop managing like a Teacher and make a personal commitment to stop hanging out in the playground. Leave School. Today. **Now.**

Stop It.

Did you stop?

Leaving School is a decision. Leave. You're allowed to. In fact, you're expected to, at some point.

Hold your Space

I love New York City and the outlook of its residents. The city may not be for everyone (although I can't understand why), but I think it's unique and incredible. Whenever I visit, I'm struck by the extent to which New Yorkers 'hold their space'. And it's brilliant.

Holding your Space means *'I'm here. I'm present. I matter and so deal with me. I have the right to be here, my opinions are relevant and you may not agree with me, but I won't be apologizing for them.'*

I love it and wish more of us held the same mentality. Holding your Space isn't about being disrespectful. It's about Confidence. People who hold their own space are entirely comfortable with you holding your space also, but they're holding theirs and not offering you any part of it. They occupy the space they're in, hold their place in it and invite you to do the same in yours.

The British mentality is often over-polite, apologizing for its existence and paranoid about causing offence. I was once in a

Starbucks on the Upper West Side and needed to use the rest room. It was busy and so as a polite, compliant Brit I formed a queue and waited patiently. Within a couple of minutes, someone arrived behind me and said 'is there someone in there?' I did what any decent Brit would do and nodded whilst raising my eyebrows and pulling a face of mock annoyance. After about 7 seconds of waiting, they pushed past me and banged on the door, shouting 'Hey, Hurry up in there! There's people in line out here!'

Now THAT's Holding your Space.

I thought about saying 'yeah, nice one. I was just about to do that actually', but then realized I was still first in the queue and instead prepared to point very clearly to the person behind me when the bathroom's current user did decide to exit and wonder who'd been chasing them. In fact, perhaps I didn't need the bathroom after all right now and so should maybe let my new friend go ahead in front of me ...

There's a big difference between a polite British tourist and a New Yorker who's holding their space.

There's a time to wait in line politely and there's a time to bang the door. Hold your Space. You have a right to be here and there's no need to apologize. And when you hold your space at work, you retain all your power and can turn it into responsibility.

You'll be pleased to know that I did get into the cubicle eventually, for what still holds the record as the fastest bathroom stop of my life.

The School Gates are Open

Deciding to leave School with Pay is the first step in developing the update to the way we perform in our chosen workplace. Once we've identified our need to update, we can start the work of developing that new way of thinking and operating; adding features and benefits, fixing issues and refreshing content. What will emerge will be a whole new version for us in the workplace; more stable, more valuable, more authentic and more alive than ever. Once we decide, we're ready to update our thinking.

Making a decision to leave is what comes first. But sometimes the challenge isn't just in recognizing the need to move on in our workplace thinking, it's in making sure we stay 'left', Holding our Space and continuing to operate outside those familiar school gates.

The harder aspect of embracing new thinking is in holding our nerve as we integrate new paradigms and behaviours. So that's what the rest of this book is about – developing an update for the Leaver in all of us, so we can finally begin Showing Up on a more regular basis; in our behaviours, in our thinking and in all of the work that we do. We need new paradigms and a new approach to reducing our water line and showing more of our Icebergs on a much more consistent basis.

Ready?

Then let's **Leave** … because the Gates are Open and we've got a whole world to Show Up in.

FIVE NEW PARADIGMS

3 billion people working across our planet.

3 billion people with 3 billion working mindsets. 3 billion plans and 3 billion sets of talents and ability. 3 billion days that will develop from 3 billion reactions, decisions and choices.

What if each of those days were 3 percent more effective? What if each of those people clocked in an improved mindset?

What if 3 billion people took their place, had a plan, played to their strengths and managed their time effectively?

What if 3 billion people finally **Showed Up**?

It would be 3 billion versions of a different remarkable. And all it would take is some updated paradigms:

~~Teacher Knows Best~~	**Think**
~~Do What You're Told~~	**Create**
~~Don't Answer Back~~	**Believe**
~~Don't Copy~~	**Connect**
~~(Play Nicely and) Stay Out of Trouble~~	**All is Well**

Think

'So how many customers have you got in this area, and what's your key demographic in this town?'

'What's your market share right now, and where does your best chance of an increase come from?'

Silence. Blank faces. Shrugging shoulders. I was with a team of area managers, responsible for over 3000 employees across more than 200 locations.

'How many people do you impact through the work you do and the decisions that are made by you as leaders in this room, this morning?'

My question prompted an unexpected discussion about parameters and boundaries, mandates and jurisdictions. I was working with leaders from the public sector who are managing multiple-million pound projects on behalf of the taxpayer.

'So what's the key message of the marketing that we see on the walls around us? What do you think it's saying to your customers? What's it telling me to expect as an individual when I buy from you?'

I was told that 'the Marketing team from head office hadn't really communicated the purpose of the new campaign'. I was with 30 retail managers, representing a household name in 30 towns and cities across the country. They'd all put the posters up anyway.

In large organizations operating under School with Pay paradigms, it's too easy to leave your brain at the door. The first paradigm of an 'updated' School Leaver, is to switch on, and to **Think**.

In fact, it's not about Switching On. It's about **Never Switching Off**.

Thought Leadership is a phrase we hear often and it is becoming an increasingly important currency in a world of growing uncertainty. Problem is, overly-hierarchical environments inflate the power and influence of the Teachers and suggest that thought leadership is the preserve of those with seniority, leaving swathes of 'students' switching off their brains and simply sitting in the classroom, waiting for inspiration from the teacher, a professor or maybe the latest guru.

Everyone can be a thought leader, just like everyone can display leadership in the right context.

Be a Thinker in your role or chosen profession, rather than waiting for the answer sheet. Below are a few short steps to making this happen:

1. Switch On

Switching on is the start … and then never switching off. Flicking our personal switches means waking up, getting engaged, getting involved and getting active.

Stop waiting for someone else to provide the answer.

Stop waiting, like a bird in a nest for someone 'bigger' to arrive with the next scrap or morsel. Get up, get out and get busy feeding yourself. Feeding yourself means reading, watching and listening to the events unfolding around you, getting informed on the circumstances in which you find yourself and surrounding yourself with people who will spark your development. Learn about your market, read influential commentators and spend time around thinking that inspires you.

Get engaged in the work you do and informed about the opportunities as they emerge and develop around you.

Wake up. Switch on. Then never switch off.

2. Understand your Business

What's the wider company plan and vision for your organization? What will success look like?

What's happening in the broader market you work in and how might that impact the strategy?

How does your business work, what are its key commercial drivers and how does your part of the business contribute to its success?

If you don't know these answers, find out. It's important.

Understanding both the broader and underlying construct of your organization allows you to take a stake in its success. Showing Up means that rather than simply being on the hook for delivering an objective or meeting a local business plan, you'll work to understand the mechanics of how it operates, the factors that drive profitability and the economics of your particular division. You'll be amazed how raising your level of attention from your direct accountabilities and responsibilities to the broader construct of the business and the contribution you're making will broaden your perspective and expand the reach of your overall impact.

3. Ask Questions, then Answer Them

What are your customers looking for? What issues do they need resolving?

What concerns do your colleagues have and what pressures are they grappling with?

How do you imagine things will look and feel around you in a few months' time or maybe a year from now? What can you start to do *now*, in order to prepare for it?

Don't wait for the issues to arise and find yourself always on the back foot and only ever reactive in your responses to resolving them. Get ahead of the game by understanding the landscape, sensing the underlying issues, spotting the opportunities and finding ways in which you can provide a solution.

And don't just ask questions. Now get active in providing the answers. Do research. Ask for advice. Do some self-study and work with others to develop fresh answers.

4. Read, Watch, Listen

This one's pretty obvious. The information we need is all around us, if we look for it:

News sites, industry publications, YouTube …

… LinkedIn, TED.com, Twitter (all great for hearing from experts you might never meet).

If you know more about the Kardashians than you do about your industry or work sector, you need to switch channels.

5. Network

We become like the people we surround ourselves with. Thinkers surround themselves with people who stretch their thinking, inspire ideas and provoke possibilities. In your own organization or team, find the people who are better at various aspects of your job than you are, and learn from them. This isn't about gathering business cards for no reason, it's focused on impact and making connections that have a purpose.

When the Teacher Knows Best paradigm becomes Think, it's *you* that Shows Up rather than someone waiting for others to do all their thinking.

Thought Leadership isn't about authority and it doesn't emerge from your structure chart. Leaving School means taking responsibility and Showing Up is about making your presence felt.

So get informed. Get active. And then get busy.

Create

In the first few months of starting my company, I was introduced to a retired Iraqi banker and entrepreneur who had fled the country in the 1960s to create a new life for his family in the UK. Abdul Karim Kattan had risen through the ranks to become General Manager of the Commercial Bank in Baghdad; a prestigious position with significant social standing. As a Shia Muslim, he later suffered and was imprisoned by the Ba'athist regime, before eventually being released and finding a way to leave the country and create a new life in the West. A serial entrepreneur with an amazing story, Kattan established a number of businesses in the UK, Europe and beyond and even in the twilight of his life still had fire in his eyes and a drive for action, a thirst for ideas and an interest in what people like me were trying to make happen. I had the privilege of spending an afternoon with Abdul Karim and his family to hear more about his life, understand his approach to starting a business and use him as an exemplar of someone who'd established a successful business that was about more than making money.

One of the many questions I asked him that afternoon was 'What's important about 'work' and the work people do?' and his answers have lived with me ever since. He began by describing one of his earliest positions in the bank as a young trainee and how he had been mentored and supervised by an experienced manager who had taken him under his wing and poured his knowledge and experience into him over a number of years. He said he owed some key aspects of his approach to work, life and business to the man who had trained him many years previously.

'A creative man is an important man. You must create.' Abdul Karim's approach and foundational belief in creativity had remained with him throughout his working life, creating opportunities, building connections and establishing companies that offered services where he'd spotted a gap in the market or seen a chance to build something entirely new. The range of activities he had found himself involved in was *wide*. He'd run a financing operation for small businesses starting up in the UK, had imported cement for a while into a community where he'd spotted a demand and at one point launched a company to manufacture a newly designed uPVC window handle, all led from his belief that all people are born to create and make a contribution to the worlds they inhabit.

A creative man is an important man. Abdul Karim's definition of 'important' was, of course, not important as we would normally understand it, as a description of position or structural authority over others 'less important' than us. This sort of important was not a graded or comparative perspective where important sought the glory and the unimportant was ignored. 'Important' to this man meant *value*, it meant *contribution* and was a word *loaded* with human potential; of what it means to be alive and a contributing member of wider society. Important meant that every person mattered, and that what we're each able to offer can make a difference to the people and circumstances and communities around us. Important is what happens when we Show Up, and so as we create, we grow into our humanity. We become who we were born to be and our presence on earth has significance and impact.

We become important because we've created and because we've contributed something.

People become important once they decide to Show Up.

So I must create. You must create. We must create.

Imagine holding **Create** as a paradigm for the work you do, from the moment you wake to when you put your head down to sleep again.

Imagine focusing your attention on taking your place in the world, on bringing what you can bring, on Showing Up in the work that you do and on making a difference through your ideas, energy and commitment to making an impact.

If *that* version of you Shows Up every day, you *will* make a difference, and according to Mr Kattan it's the only thing that's really of any long-term importance. There won't be many Teachers on the scene for those sort of people's thinking.

Abdul Karim Kattan lived and worked his whole career with a foundational paradigm that making something happen would define his 'importance' and therefore value as an individual. And far from being fearful, small-minded and risk averse, he was alive, confident and still open to the opportunities that presented themselves in every interaction. His presence was compelling. He was a man I'd have followed.

So a drive for creativity isn't fearful. It doesn't glance over its shoulder. It faces clear forward and doesn't hand power to others. Create scans for opportunities and always looks to build something, do something or establish something that might just make a difference to each and every one of us.

Creating is an instinct that reminds us we're alive.

Creativity takes effort and yet often works with a smile on its face.

As we drank tea together that memorable afternoon, I was struck by the extent to which my host's attention was external; on other people and situations and rarely concerned with himself. He struggled to answer questions directly concerning his own opinions, preferring instead to reveal them through the stories of those he'd supported, colleagues he'd worked with or companies he'd built partnerships with. His identity was in the difference he'd made, the things and ways he'd contributed to others and the broader result of the projects and ventures he'd put effort into. Here was a man who in the final quarter of his life on this planet, was looking back on his contribution not as a series of 'I' statements or as a CV of personal achievements, but rather through the people he'd professionally encountered, the family he'd provided for and the needs that had been met in the communities he'd been part of.

The world seemed small to him and its possibilities endless and one of the many things I noticed was how often he sat chuckling.

Imagine the ways in which your working experience could be transformed by adding Create as a working paradigm. Who could stop you if you thought like that?

Imagine if you judged your value by what you'd created; by what was growing or changing or developing or evolving and which made a difference to your customers, colleagues or stakeholders, rather than assessing your salary level, job grade or your position in the overall company performance curve.

Imagine if you told stories at your performance review of the ways you'd been 'important' through the people you'd impacted and the success of others rather than your own personal achievements.

Imagine if your performance review was all about others, and that you rarely used the word 'I'.

Imagine if you took it one step further and in fact allowed your impact to tell your story, rather than resorting to Show and Tell whenever someone important hasn't noticed you. We probably wouldn't know quite what to do with you and yet you'd probably still be smiling ...

Here are some pointers that I picked up from Abdul Karim that will help you to Create and be *his* version of Important:

Be Ready. You're not going to Show Up very well or very often if you're sleeping.

Be Present. Get involved. It's the workplace equivalent of bouncing on your toes, ready to respond to shots from all directions. Switch on, get alert and have the stance of someone in action.

Ask (More!) Questions. Find out what others really want and need, whether customers, colleagues or the people who work for you. Spend more time on this bit than in chalking up the answer for them. Shift your attention to their needs and understand what going on for them in detail. You'll need more than one good question before diving into a solution.

Listen. I know someone who asks pretty good questions and yet never really listens to hear a developing answer. Eventually, people stop replying. It's like making a great tennis serve and bowing to the crowd for the finesse with which you executed it, blissfully ignorant of the return whistling past your ear. People don't win much this way. When you ask questions, stick around long enough to understand the answers.

Be Generous. Once you understand the problem (or opportunity?!), look for ways to get stuck in and get useful. Who have you helped recently? Who have you given support to pro bono? Which people are more supported, more successful, more fulfilled and more developed because they found you in their orbit recently? Oh, and before you write a press release, take a glance at the next point.

Stand at the Back. You'd walk past Mr Kattan in the street. There was nothing about him that would see him centre stage of any performance, but he talked all afternoon about the businesses, ventures, partnerships and opportunities he'd created and when I came away that evening, I knew I'd only scratched the surface. Let others be the fire from the spark you've provided. **People who are _really_ important don't tend to need others to notice it.**

I love the idea of importance being something that comes from impact and its results in the wider world and community, rather than being anything to do with our qualifications, intellect, credentials or authority level.

If each of us can be important, then all our personal contributions matter. And because we have potential, there's now plenty of room for each of us to walk into it.

You don't need a higher position, more authority or a bigger budget sign off. No-one's important just because they sit above you on a structure chart. That's not Important. Important is what will be measured by the *impact* you've had and where you've helped every one of us. And that's got nothing to do with the wording of your job title.

Outside of school rules, a *truly* important person is a creative person. You must Create.

Believe (in Your Power)

I woke up and knew exactly what to do. It was either a dream or early-morning inspiration (ever get that?), but it was vivid and clear and I wanted to start immediately. It was about a skate park. It would be a local venue, where skaters would be welcome. It would be a central gathering place and somewhere we could call home. And it wouldn't be easy.

In 1996 and in my mid-twenties, I took a brief career break to become a youth worker, launching a project called Tribe in the South East of England. It was a transformational experience (and more on that later). On this particular morning, I'd been working on Tribe for about a year or so and had felt for a while that we needed a big idea we could pin everything on. Tribe needed to be a different sort of youth provision but I still hadn't worked out how. In the UK at the time, skate culture was experiencing another end-of-decade renaissance. Sony's new Playstation console seemed to be changing all our lives and, although it would be another 18 months before Tony Hawk released his first skate game into the market, from where I was lying that morning the timing was perfect. I wanted a warehouse. I wanted a skate park, offices and a couple of units for local young adults to start their own businesses. All this, despite having no money and not a clue what I was about to be doing.

Pete lived on the South Coast and was doing great things to support young people in his own town. I'd made a point of spending time with him occasionally; sharing ideas, discussing current issues and generally getting inspiration for what I was trying to create back home. I shared my idea of the skate venue and, needless to say, Pete got it. A few months later, having searched in vain for appropriate and affordable venues, been misunderstood by the local council and struggling to develop a coherent business plan, I found myself in a slump. I spent an evening at Pete's place and just before I left, he gave it to me.

It was a bright purple skate deck, which had never been ridden on. No grip tape, no trucks, no wheels and no bearings. It was basically a carved piece of wood, but we both knew what it represented for me at that time. It didn't work as a skateboard – yet. But we both knew it would and that I'd eventually ride it. One day.

On the deck was the graffiti rendering of a word we'd discussed just a few weeks before … Apostle. The word comes from an Old French derivation of the Greek word 'apostolos' and is probably most recognizable to us as the title given to saints like Peter and Paul. An apostle is simply someone who pioneers or is entrusted with a mission. The skate park was my mission and as a team we definitely felt entrusted with it. The next day, I nailed the deck to the wall of my office, right above my desk. From now on, I'd see it every time I went to work; a reminder of what I was here for and the purpose I was involved in.

Eventually, after more failed attempts to purchase a local building, we decided to run a one-off event in a local leisure centre over Christmas. Under the leadership of Keith, my ever-up-for-it project manager, we built a skate park from scratch in just a few days. Push '99 was a pre-Christmas skate festival, sponsored by Playstation, which hosted a number of DJs, a couple of skate teams and the current national streetdance champions. We had absolutely no idea what we were doing.

Pre-Facebook, pre-Twitter and with very little marketing, we had over 2000 kids through that first park over just a few days and it was the most tiring, exciting and scary thing I'd ever done. Push was an amazing success, with a team of dedicated volunteers delivering something that had at many times seemed impossible, but that we'd managed through blood, sweat and tears to make a reality. Push events developed into a small local events company and within three years the town would have its own outdoor park, opposite the site of that very first weekend. I doubt any of it would have happened without us.

A great experience, but my most significant memory was in a few quiet moments just before the park opened. I went back to my car and pulled out the Apostle deck. It had never been set up, had never been ridden and in fact up until that point hadn't even been stood on. It had been on my office wall, waiting for the moment when that early morning idea had finally become reality.

It was a moment that lives with me and which I've never forgotten; a few precious moments riding the park on my own, skating over the ramps and making my way up and down every line. I was probably the least proficient skater to ride the park that weekend, but each memorable second was a chance to drink in the atmosphere and reflect on the sights, sounds and smells all around me. Ramps, barriers, stickers and turntables and upright Playstation consoles playing games that are now history.

This was what I'd seen when I'd woken up that morning all those months before. *This* was a local skate park and the idea that I'd thought of. Although it wasn't exactly how I'd imagined it and there had definitely been set-backs, on a day like today, none of that even mattered. This *was* a skate park and it *did* exist in reality; a mission we had been on that *made* Christmas for local skaters. Almost two years and a dream now fulfilled.

Those twenty short minutes at the end of 1999 have become the anchor for my personal **Believe** paradigm. Anchoring describes the experience you have when you play an old piece of music or taste Mum's classic cake recipe and feel as though you've been transported back to the exact time and place where those things happened originally. It's why nostalgia is so powerful and why we reconnect with school friends on Facebook. We create anchors for various emotional states all the time and, of course, some of them aren't always helpful for us. Waking up to hear rain falling against the window can become a negative anchor if we choose to carry it around with us all day.

Our minds and emotions can be incredibly powerful for us, when we're intentional in our state management and exercise control and choice over the emotions that we're experiencing.

Anchoring in a conscious way is a simple technique in recalling emotional states that will be most useful to us as we go about our lives and in given situations, e.g. when we need confidence, clarity, presence or calm. Most of us have experienced memorable moments in our lives, when we have just felt fantastic or the world has seemed well with us. Anchoring can help us carry those moments with us and make them present and useful in our current conscious minds. I wish they'd taught us **that** when we were at school.

When we recall them, we can choose to 'turn up' our senses on the best of our experiences; either making colours more vivid, sounds crisper or allowing the feelings we were feeling to grow more within us. It feels amazing and our brains relive it as though it's happening again in reality – a natural high. The process of anchoring those states is also pretty simple. Like putting on the record or biting into Mum's sponge cake, a simple physical action can act as a trigger for an emotional state in the future. Some people rub their fingers together, others breathe in deeply, and some clear their throats or maybe scratch their ears.

Part of my Believe paradigm is anchored in that first skate festival. No matter what happens in my personal future, the Push weekend **happened**. It's a fact. A skate park *was* built, my dream *was* realized and it's now part of my history, part of my story and a contribution that made a difference. Whether you're my client, a director, a CEO or the President – in Christmas 1999 I made something happen, which for me is powerful. It resides in my DNA, it cannot be removed from me and means I can engage with authority, structure and seniority without letting those things define me or my reactions in the moment. It means I have value. It means I can be confident. It means I can be present and fully own the power of that experience, removing any need to compete or compare myself with other people around me.

Anchoring your best moments means carrying them with you in the times you most need them; and when you have a Believe paradigm, the power of your experiences will always be available to you.

Try Believe for yourself:

- Remember a moment when you felt **fantastic**. Remember when you felt at your best – maybe a time when you were with those who are closest to you, or a positive and life-changing event you've experienced, or when you achieved a significant goal that you'd set for yourself.
- Remind yourself of the things that have happened and that are now part of your story.
- Take some time to remember the scene, just as if it was a film being played on a screen in front of you.
- Now turn up the volume, turn up the colour and step into the picture. Pay attention to how you begin feeling.
- Notice how powerful the memory is and how resourceful and confident you begin to feel. And remember, this happened, it's real and it's part of your story.

Why would you hand that over or let anyone take it away from you? **Believe in your Power.**

Remember, you're [insert your name]. No-one can take your very best away from you.

At some point when you're alone, find yourself a mirror. You won't be able to resist this once you've read it. Look deep into the reflection of your very own eyes, and repeat after me:

I'm [insert name], who the hell are you?

If you want to, repeat it. I bet you smile.

Connect

A few years ago, I took a number of trips to the fabulously named Mountain Kingdom of Lesotho. Lesotho is a small land-locked enclave of South Africa; a beautiful part of the world that's created great memories. It was during my time in Lesotho and South Africa in the late 1990s that I discovered *Ubuntu*.

Ubuntu might be familiar to you as the open-source Linux operating system, although the Ubuntu I discovered was the spirit and philosophy from which that software took its name. Ubuntu is a term derived from the Bantu group of languages, which can essentially be translated as *'I am what I am because of who we all are.'*

In 2008, Archbishop Desmond Tutu described Ubuntu as *'the essence of being human. Ubuntu speaks particularly about the fact that you can't exist as a human being in isolation. It speaks about our interconnectedness. You can't be human all by yourself, and when you have this quality – Ubuntu – you are known for your generosity. We think of ourselves far too frequently as just individuals, separated from one another, whereas you are connected and what you do affects the whole world. When you do well, it spreads out; it is for the whole of humanity.'*

In Ubuntu, the priority is connection rather than individuality and a simple way to understand this is in the construct of a basic conversation. Generally, when we converse in the West, we **Stack**. In Lesotho and other cultures with a strong tribal foundation, they **Circle**. Think about the way a conversation tends to develop between colleagues, friends or occasional acquaintances.

The conversation starts with one person telling a story:

'The traffic was really bad last night.'

The person who's listening now 'stacks' on the comment they've heard:

'Last night? Well, you should have seen it last week, I've never seen anything like it.'

The original story-teller now has a choice – to either hear more of the newly-stacked story, or raise the stakes personally, with their own slightly bigger one:

'Well the worst journey I ever had on that road was when I had to sleep in the car overnight ... now that *was* crazy ...'

Do you recognize this shape to some of your conversations? Listen out for it next time you hear small-talk, or people supposedly chatting to each other. The risk with a Stacked conversation is that neither person listens effectively. Each member of the conversation is simply waiting for a break or someone to take a breath in order to trump the speaker with their own, ever-so-slightly-more-impressive story. Under the guise of 'building rapport' and 'having a natter', those involved have established an unspoken competition where at the end of this conversation, there'll eventually be a 'winner'.

Notice this next time you see four or five work colleagues out for a drink ... the ritualized conversations and back-and-forth banter are likely to consist of a series of Stacks, until some order is established and everyone relaxes into the environment.

In more tribal cultures, the conversation is Circular, meaning the focus is on everyone contributing and with the clock reset after each person has spoken. There's no competition, and each comment stands on its own merit. The aim is to hear from you, not see if we can do better. When each person speaks, the rest of the group listens, and then the next person speaks and offers their perspective. The spirit of a Circle conversation has its base in the ancient protocols of an elder's council, a leadership round-table or a campfire circle. In these environments, the question is more important than the answer and the power of a developing conversation more valuable than its conclusion.

Circular conversations retain the spirit of Ubuntu ... a conversation can only be truly described as one in the context of what we've *all* contributed to it.

Nancy Kline suggests a similar concept in her book *A Time to Think*, where she describes 'listening meetings', where people are given the time and opportunity to explore their thoughts in full without someone else jumping in to correct them, react to what they've said or piggy-back their contribution. Having experimented with this sort of meeting protocol myself, it's entirely counter-cultural and yet regularly more fulfilling. You'd be amazed what it's like to take part in a meeting where all contributions are equally valued and where you can talk far more freely, knowing you won't be interrupted.

In 2000, I organized a team of young people to visit Lesotho to build a school for street children in Motimposo, a small community on the outskirts of the capital, Maseru. It was on this trip that I'd see Ubuntu in action. Our trip was to support a local free school offer, started by an inspirational man called Michael Kolisang, who worked among the community and had launched a host of other projects. Our plan was to prepare and lay foundations for two pre-built units, which we'd specified from the UK and would bring in from South Africa. We'd be on the ground with a five-day window. With a few adult helpers (including Annie, my wonderful PA at the time, who'd lived in Lesotho for a couple of years with her husband Julian and young family), we arrived from Johannesburg with a van full of hormonal teenagers, all unaware of quite what was facing them.

Our preparations had been made from the UK in a time that was pre-email, pre-Skype and therefore pre-FaceTime, so consisted of scribbled faxes and occasional broken phone calls, all designed to line up as much as possible ahead of our arrival. The existing school building was a small unused dwelling in the north-east corner of a rectangular plot of land that Michael had acquired. Our plan was pretty simple: to excavate foundations for the two new units across the southern end of the plot, then demolish the existing building when the new structures were in place and operational. Or so we thought.

When we arrived, there was real excitement in the community and, as always, we received the sort of welcome I've only ever had in that country.

Then we visited the site for the first time.

It wasn't quite what we were expecting. The plot of land was a bomb site. The 'old' school building had already been demolished, meaning the school had been closed, awaiting the amazing new buildings. Maybe that explained the even-better-than-usual welcome. But there was another problem. The rubble from the old building was now directly in the spot we'd ear-marked for the new buildings.

Day 1 in the Big Brother House. Tim, is stressing out in the garden …

Getting hold of heavy machinery at short notice over a weekend proved challenging and eventually we reverted to what was probably plan F, buying a box-load of gloves and a truck load of shovels and deciding to clear an area we could at least get started with. Clearing rubble just to start digging foundations wasn't a factor in my finely tuned plan and none of the team were remotely like labourers. It wasn't any of us at our best, as we adjusted to the heat and quickly fell behind schedule. I felt pretty annoyed and despite being team leader, was struggling to stay positive.

I was digging away, shifting as much as I could handle and keeping my real thoughts to myself, when I noticed two hands scratching away at the red dirt beside me. I turned, to be met by a middle-aged local woman in tired, dirty clothing, shifting the earth by hand into a bucket just beside her. I reacted quickly and instinctively, trying to make her stop and explaining through an interpreter that we had gloves and shovels and she might get hurt by helping. *Leave it to us, it's what we all came over here for.*

She stared back at me with a face full of purpose and without blinking said in Sotho, 'My son will come to this school.'

And with that she turned, and continued her digging.

Ubuntu. We are who we are because of who we all are.

That day, I got it. I finally understood what we were really all there for. Yes it was about a building, yes it was about five days, and yes we were under pressure and our plan was unravelling, but this wasn't about heroes and a Hollywood backing track. **It was about this community and the children who were growing in it.** It was about trying to make things better for someone, and we'd be a few words in a much longer chapter. It was about our common purpose and everyone throwing in together, about forgetting personal preferences and just doing whatever it took to give these children a building. Our project became a purpose and its success would be measured in the context of all of us.

I learnt more about project management in those five days than in the previous twelve years of working. I'm pretty sure that a short interaction in a pile of African rubble changed parts of me forever and definitely my attention.

By the time we left, the foundations had been laid and Eagle's Nest School in Motimposo would have two new buildings to take it forward. And, as ever, each of us had received something of far more value than anything our shovels had managed when we were digging with them.

A paradigm to Connect creates Organizational Ubuntu.

Imagine if the divisions of your company focused around a purpose that was truly co-dependent and where success was experienced when it was realized in all of us. Imagine if the Sales division and Projects teams, or IT and Marketing groups operated on the basis that they only had an identity in the context of what they were *ALL* delivering. And isn't that what we're all supposed to be doing anyway?

Imagine if an organization's group purpose really could become more valuable than localized preferences.

Imagine if the department heads across your organization had circular conversations to drive success rather than Stacking each other in weekly Show and Tell.

It might be utopian, or it could just be an Update. It might be dreamland, or a more effective paradigm.

And Organizational Ubuntu is not corporate coffee and cuddles. Let's look again at Bishop Tutu's description: '...the essence of **being human** ... you **can't exist in isolation** ... our **interconnectedness** ... you are known for **generosity** ... what you do affects the whole world ... it is for the **whole of humanity**.'

Take a look back at those words and apply them in your organization:

- What does *humanity* look like for the way you serve customers and operate internally?
- Where might your team be *isolated*, and missing out on commercial opportunities?
- How does your company in some way *make the world better* and how does it affect the way you perform when you're doing a job in it?

Your organization *could* begin to grapple with Organizational Ubuntu; you *could* take on Connect as a paradigm for the work you do. And please don't tell me it wouldn't have commercial value, or serve to make your customers happier or drive overall brand loyalty.

What would it take for your organization to be so clear on its culture and intent, its beliefs and its purpose, that everyone was working for the whole group's objective rather than silently pursuing localized agendas?

Or for the very basis on which you operated to be one of inclusion and in seeking out the value of everyone's contribution, rather than competition that turns in on itself, game-playing and covering answer papers?

Or where collaboration wasn't just an aspirational buzz-word, but a philosophy we believed and really showed we worked from?

- To Connect is to understand the 'group value' of everyone around us and to take each other's talent seriously enough to throw our efforts in with them without holding back or spectating.
- To Connect means we're only successful in a context of all of us. We can only be a team through the evidence of behaving like one. And everyone matters and has a voice to be listened to.
- To Connect means we want to Show Up and that our corporate success is on each of us working this way.

Ubuntu might not be easy, but it can be done. And instinctively it's something we can't afford to ignore. It might be a challenging paradigm, but in case you forgot, **School with Pay isn't working.**

Compare Organizational Ubuntu with Corporate Show and Tell.

You can give me the campfire and meeting in a Circle anytime.

All is Well

Dr Eben Alexander is an American academic neurosurgeon who has taught at Harvard Medical School, along with hospital appointments at the Brigham and Women's and the Children's Hospital in Boston, Massachusetts.

In 2008, Alexander contracted meningitis and fell gravely ill, spending a week in a coma at the Lynchburg General Hospital in Virginia. In his 2012 New York Times Bestseller *Proof of Heaven*, he describes his near death experience (NDE) during that week, prior to waking up and making a full and remarkable recovery. His account of his NDE and what he describes (as a previously sceptical scientist) as 'heaven' have been the source of some debate, although personally I was most struck by the first words he said when he emerged from his coma, with his family sat around him:

All is Well.

All is Well – these are the perfect words for a fifth new paradigm. What would work be like, if rather than holding a (Play Nicely and) Stay Out of Trouble paradigm, we acted as though All was Well?

When All is Well, there's no 'trouble' to get into. All is Well is the polar opposite of Fear. And as we'll discover, when we're fearless, what's the worst that can happen?! When All is Well, we don't have to fight, be jealous, resent others or 'play nasty' in order to make our presence felt because, well, All … Is … Well.

Think about it for a moment. If you really acted in your job as though All really *was* Well, how might it be different? What would the impact be on your actions, your reactions and the ways in which you operated?

Too many of us work as though All is *Not* Well or that 'all is unlikely to be well, so don't get your hopes up' or as if 'all might be well now but don't rest for a moment because it'll turn in a moment and bite you'. And it doesn't seem to make us happy. It doesn't help us trust people, it can make us risk averse and leave us always expecting the down-side of every opportunity. Thinking as though all isn't well might be very realistic, pragmatic and 'experienced', but it rarely boosts performance or makes for a great team dynamic.

All is Well is an incredible paradigm to work by. It's an empowering, encouraging and life-affirming mantra. It means that we *matter*; it means that we're *valued* and it means that we don't have to work with one eye over our shoulders.

When All is Well, you can work more confidently, bringing your contribution and allowing your life and talents to shine through in the work you do. Think about the moments when your work has gone well or you've received fantastic feedback or know that some work you've done has made a positive difference to someone. In those moments, however brief and fleeting, you'll have experienced what it's like to know that All is Well.

All is Well doesn't have to be temporary. It could be a paradigm for the way you work from this day forward.

When you Think, Create, Believe, Connect and then live your working life as if All is Well, your attention is on outcomes, on *life* and on possibility. When you apply your talents, your intellect and competencies to the work you do, no organization or individual can 'hold' you and you don't need to hand over any more power. Free from the need to compete for position or recognition, your attention will be on all you have to offer, you'll communicate with confidence and display the potential of your Iceberg.

When All is Well, we can Show Up freely, because, well, why wouldn't we? There's no longer a reason not to and the distractions in our mindset from delivering peak performance have been removed and so we'll start Showing Up in a world that's always been there, waiting for us.

All is Well doesn't ignore life's challenges. It doesn't pretend that bad things don't happen, or that clouds don't appear, bringing rain on a regular basis, but it does define our reactions to them and the state of our minds as we navigate our working existence.

All is Well is a working paradigm, not an emotion. It's a way of thinking or a frame for understanding the working world around us. And rather than 'staying out' of the 'trouble' that's all around us, it chooses to think differently, and in some strange way, even sometimes in the midst of the opposite, all *can* still be well. All is Well is a paradigm that takes back control for yourself in your reactions, emotions and your choices for how you conduct yourself professionally. As we've seen already, School with Pay hands control to others, inflating their authority and diminishing our own options and power in the process. All is Well means you begin to call the shots again. This is *your* life, *your* career, *your* professional journey and to allow it to be defined or unhelpfully influenced by other people or persons is a distortion of reality. Which means *it isn't true.*

All *is* Well. And so work begins to feel different – an expression of your talents and your value as an individual. All is Well drops the waterline around your Iceberg, and you can begin again to bring your best, be your best and think your best when the alarm goes off, however early in the morning.

Just try it for a moment. Take a deep breath in, then let it go and say to yourself with conviction:

'All. Is. Well.'

Repeat it, often.

When All is Well, Who Needs Balance?

When All is Well in the way we frame the work we do, many of the restrictions of our made-up thinking begin to fall away and the lines between work and life can finally be blurred again. Compare a paradigm that All is Well with the age-old search for a work/life balance ...

Balance suggests that there are things in play that oppose each other, and which must be carefully organized to establish equilibrium. Balance suggests a tension of some sort or a framework teetering on the edge of impending disaster. *Balance* sounds like the equivalent of the worst sort of family Christmas, with each of the combustible family members seated carefully around the table and with certain members separated, to avoid potential conflict or explosion. Like alkali elements reacting with water, 'maintaining a careful balance' sounds like effort that's unnecessary.

- Whoever said that work and life were in opposition to each other, that they were enemies and that we had to establish a balance between them?
- Who decided that work and life were descriptions of two opposites and that they didn't really get on with each other?

Think about the words 'work/life balance' for a moment. The categorizations of this statement suggest that the work we do is somehow distinct from the 'real' lives that we lead, or that life itself is separate from the work we do. Separating work and life as though they're two separate entities creates in itself a barrier of our own making.

In one sentence, we've told ourselves that our work is somehow different to 'real life' and that, in reverse, 'real life' can't exist in the presence of the 'work' we do. **It's rubbish, isn't it?** No wonder some of us are on auto-pilot and have allowed School with Pay to thrive unchallenged.

I don't believe in creating a work/life balance. I believe in creating a great Life.

I don't want a *balance* between my life and my work, because they're not in opposition to each other. I'm interested in creating a full and fulfilling life for myself and with those I have around me, in grasping hold of every moment and squeezing the juice out of it, regardless of whether it pays me or not. I choose **Life**, which includes work, boredom, joy, frustration, excitement, setbacks and a heart that beats every second.

If you're in a job that's in opposition to the life you want or if the life that's in you can't be reflected in the job you do, change your paradigms and the way you're thinking about them. And if, once you've done that, your life and your work are still in conflict, one of them needs to change.

Change your life, change your job or change whatever's put them both in a place of opposition, because if All is Well, they really don't have to be.

When all is well, Life involves Work and Work involves Life. And that doesn't sound like something that needs 'balancing'.

A New Game

By updating the paradigms that are driving your working mindset, you can begin to experience a full life on a whole new basis; full of creativity and learning, connection and confidence, with the end result that All remains Well. I think people working this way probably laugh more freely and will definitely be having more fun when you meet them at a party.

Is All is Well something I've made up? Yes. It is.

Of course it's made up, but it's also an entirely new game for our thinking; one that looks for the positive, re-states we're alive and refuses to give power to external influences.

When All is Well, we smile more often. When All is Well, we all hold our heads high.

Think
Believe
Create
Connect
All is Well.

Five new paradigms, for an entirely new working mindset.

Now *that* sounds like a work-style or life-work that's worth waking for …

BRINGING YOUR MOST – FOUR GEARS FOR SHOWING UP

Four Gears for Showing Up

Alongside five new paradigms, there are four components that will help you transition the way you approach your work. Making a tangible shift across each of them will reframe, update and change your outlook on the work you do, the behaviours you display whenever you clock in and the way your professional life sits within the broader frame of your time on this planet. Rebuilding each aspect will put you outside the school gates of your thinking and help you integrate new paradigms for your working life moving forward.

Four components that make a School Leaver. Four components to help you Show Up.

They're concerned with revealing you 'at your MOST'; your Most resourceful, your Most enterprising, your Most present and your Most impactful. Your at your MOST is likely to be pretty close to the person we met at your interview. You at your MOST was what got you the job offer, because in any good interview, there's no teacher and no playground, just a few great questions that revealed something like the best of you.

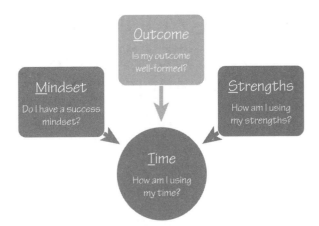

Figure 2: MOST Performance Model

Being at your MOST is about giving attention to your thinking, your planning, your talents and your performance (see the model in Figure 2). It's about your **Mindset**, your **Outcomes**, your **Strengths** and how you spend your **Time** ...

Our developing Mindset and the way we understand and apply our personal Strengths directly impacts the quality and efficacy of the plans we make (our Outcomes) and the combination of these three aspects will be manifested in the way we spend the Time we have available.

If I followed you around for a few days while you were working, I'd get a pretty good read on the ways your mindset, outcomes and strengths were in play from the way you spent your time and what you did or didn't give attention to. Your time is where all three are manifested (or not). You can't improve the way you relate to time without improving the way you think, plan and utilize your abilities. And you can't make a shift in your thinking, planning or ability without your schedule being on board to make it happen.

Mindset, Outcomes, Strengths and Time.

You, at your MOST.

Attending to each element will help you integrate your new paradigms and be more effective in Showing Up through the work you do.

Let's go.

GEAR 1 – YOUR MINDSET

The Success Mindset

It *can't* be done.

It *won't* get authorized.

They *might* not like it.

That *isn't* the way it works around here.

Because they're driven by fear and a skewed way of reacting to organizational power, School with Pay reactions are nearly always **negative**, along with their impact on us and the people we're working with.

The next time you use a can't, won't, shouldn't or isn't, have a quick check to see if the schoolyard's lurking somewhere in your mindset. And as we've seen already, it's easy for our minds to play tricks on us. Our attention, our energy and our reactions to what's happening around us will determine the directions we find ourselves heading in, and our minds can run wild if we don't take control of them or make good choices about where they're taking us.

Our minds deserve effort and attention, because they'll *always* determine the places we'll go.

It's our minds that convince us that our thoughts are real and that our opinions are correct. It's our minds that tell us our reactions describe things that are *actually* happening, rather than simply being our own personal response to the events unfolding around us. When you pull out in front of me when I'm driving on the motorway and I call you an idiot, is it *true* or is it just my reaction, in the heat of the moment and given a certain set of circumstances?

It's also our minds that talk to us about ourselves, describing to us our own personal value and settling on our behalf our place in the working world around us. Some of the words they speak would be better unspoken.

It's too easy for us to make stuff up in our minds and in our thinking ... and then act as if what we've created is all true.

And **Updates are Available**. Always. For all of us.

Think back to the five paradigms. A paradigm is simply a construct of basic assumptions or ways of thinking. One dictionary definition describes it as a 'cognitive framework shared by members of a discipline or group'. A paradigm is a set of assumptions, a shared way of thinking or a mindset that a group of people buy into.

A paradigm is not Truth. It's a construct and a belief system, not a reflection of absolute reality.

As we've seen with the School with Pay paradigms, ways of thinking sometimes need shifting. A paradigm shift is a dramatic, significant or approach-altering change to a previously adopted way of thinking. It's quite literally an entirely new mindset in relation to an old subject. It's a world-changing Update. A paradigm shift can be transformational and ground-breaking and has the power to break down the walls of a previously adopted mindset. When we undergo a paradigm shift, we're able to see that the world is different and often bigger and better and more open and full of possibility than all the ways we've been previously thinking about it.

Paradigm shifts change *everything*.

Sting's 1996 album *Mercury Falling* included a track called 'I Was Brought to My Senses', where he explores a lover's epiphany as they wonder how to pursue another. He describes the moment as 'a veil being removed from their eyes', with a sudden clarity that they've been walking blind 'now that they can see'.

School with Pay is a metaphor that might just bring *us* to our senses. Understanding the games we've been playing shows us the ways we've been blind to outdated thinking and behaviours and so now we can begin to see our lives and the purpose of our work differently. And out of what was confusion, a new mindset fired by entirely new paradigms is emerging, that will help us see a few things that really *are* true, and which might have been there all along.

Your Mindset *can* be Positive.

It *can* be Possible.

It *can* be Empowering.

It *can* do you Good.

A few thoughts below, to spark a shift in your working mindset:

No Failure, Only Feedback

'No Failure, Only Feedback' is an often-used mantra that I review in our performance programmes, asking people to apply a RAG code (rating it as Red (disagree), Green (agree) or Amber (not sure) from their experiences). I'm amazed at the number of leaders who are drawn to the word 'failure' and almost celebrate it as a label to use when 'driving a team forward' or 'getting people to work in the real world'.

'People fail – deal with it.'

'Don't get all warm and fluffy on us, get *real*.'

'It's a cruel world out there Tim, there are winners and losers …'

Of course, it's not about the words on their own – it's about what they say about our attention.

How would you rate No Failure, Only Feedback as a statement?

Which F-word do you give the most attention to?

In April 2011, Rory McIlroy competed in the US Masters, one of golf's four Major tournaments, held each year at the famous Augusta National Golf Club. For three of the four days, Northern Ireland's newest golfing superstar played incredible golf and seemed on target to win his first Major. He began his fourth and final round with a four-stroke lead at 12 under par. The competition was his to lose.

After nine holes, he was 11 strokes under par, his lead now cut to a single stroke. Only a single stroke but still the lead golfer in the tournament. And then he walked onto the tenth tee.

As has happened to many great players over the years on the final nine holes and the last day of the Masters, a triple-bogey 7 on the tenth triggered a collapse, where he'd drop three more shots over the next two holes and slump to an 8 over par final round of 80. Rory McIlroy left the Augusta National having finished at just 4 under par and in an overall tie for 15th place in the tournament.

The sports headlines, phone-ins and back pages the following morning were astonishing.

'CHOKER ...'

'One of the biggest MELTDOWNS in golfing history ...'

'COLLAPSE of a Master ...'

'Is this the END for Rory ...?'

'DISASTER on the 10th Tee ...'

One phone-in in the UK featured an expert in 'the science of choking', with many golf commentators speculating on 'whether we would ever see this young man competing at the highest level in the sport again ...'

Rory McIlroy was 21 years old.

I follow Rory on Twitter. He's normally upbeat, looks like he's having fun and is an interesting person to hear from. After the Masters he went quiet for a while. And then finally he tweeted:

'Well that wasn't the plan! Found it tough going today, but you have to lose before you can win. This day will make me stronger in the end.'

No Failure, Only Feedback?

McIlroy later tweeted a photo of himself posing with the tournament winner, South African Charl Schwartzel, as they shared a plane to their next tournament in Malaysia. Schwartzel was wearing the famous green jacket, presented to each winner of the US Masters; the *very* jacket that McIlroy could and, according to some, *should* have been wearing, along with the comment:

'Flying to Malaysia with Charl! Glad one of us has a green jacket on!!!'

Which RAG code would Rory McIlroy give our well known mantra?

Next time something goes badly for you or doesn't work out the way you'd planned, 'try on' Rory McIlroy's reaction to his final round experience at The Masters and ask yourself *his* questions:

- What did I learn?
- What valuable information do I now have, that will help me next time?
- What have I now experienced that I can integrate for a better performance the next time I face a similar challenge, problem or set-back?

It's not that 'failure' in itself doesn't exist. I doubt Rory McIlroy's plan going into the 2011 Masters was to lead for 63 holes before dropping back to 15th place. 15th was *not* the plan.

Failure exists. Failure is real. But where our attention goes and what we do next is what defines the lasting impact those experiences have on us. McIlroy's attention wasn't on 15th place. It wasn't on his tee shot at the tenth and it wasn't on the green jacket that he wouldn't be wearing (yet).

Rory McIlroy wasn't looking at the end of his skis.

What he *was* looking at was what he'd learned. He was focused on how he'd developed and grown from the experience; both factors that would help him make adjustments the next time he was in the same position, because in his mind, there *would* be a next time. McIlroy took the learning, took the feedback, took the experience and integrated it into his game.

He made it part of his story.

Choking was entirely made up by his all-wise observers. It wasn't Rory McIlroy's truth.

When asked by a reporter what he'd learned on that final day, he replied: 'This is my first experience at it, and hopefully the next time I'm in this position, I'll be able to handle it a little better ... It was a character-building day. Put it that way. I'll come out stronger for it.'

From Choker to Champion

On 19 June 2011, and at the next Major tournament of the season, Rory McIlroy won the US Open championship at the Congressional Country Club, Maryland, with a record low score of 268, 16 strokes under par.

He was the youngest US Open champion since Bobby Jones in 1923. His winning margin was eight shots, the same number as he'd dropped in the final round at Augusta two months earlier. He became a multiple major winner the following year, when he won the US PGA Championship at Kiawah Island, South Carolina, by another record eight strokes.

There's no failure, only feedback. Just ask Rory.

Hunt down the development that's available every time you have a 'failure'.

What will *you* do the next time you drop eight shots on the final day of a big tournament? You can focus on the failure, or give attention to the feedback it's offering you. What conditions caused the situation? What decisions and behaviour contributed to the result? Why did you react the way you did? What have you learned about yourself? What will you do differently next time?

Look for the learning rather than avoiding the Teachers. *Your* US Open might be two short months away.

Being Fearless

'What's the worst that could happen ...?'

Most of us have seen this slogan on a bottle of Dr Pepper, along with the great adverts, which led off with this innocent question and finished in carnage and mayhem. I guess we all laugh at them, but how often do we live as though they were true?

I once had a client who was financially secure well before retirement and yet was working harder than ever. They were working in a team (and not leading it) and loving every minute. From our short conversation, I noticed the way they were talking; their energy and enthusiasm. Every word seemed positive, they often talked about the future and their attention was on possibilities, on connections and adventures.

And they smiled. A lot.

Their energy was infectious and I realized there was something even more attractive about them ... they were Fearless. They weren't worried about how they would look or the impact of a possible failure on their reputation. They weren't 'scared what the teacher might think' and they certainly weren't thinking about 'the worst that could happen'.

Have you ever met someone who was fearless at work? Really *fear-LESS*?

What was your reaction to them? Were you intimidated by them? Jealous? Was being around them a little uncomfortable? What does that tell you ... and have you ever worked this way?

How about this from Michael Jordan, arguably the best basketball player of all time and one of the biggest names in the sport:

> *I've missed more than 9000 shots in my career. I've lost almost 300 games. 26 times, I've been trusted to take the game winning shot and missed. I've failed over and over and over again in my life. And that is why I succeed.*

No failure, only feedback. No fear, just experience.

Jordan played Fearless. He played loose. He played with freedom. He kept on shooting. And the confidence in his eyes often had the opposition beaten before the starter's clock turned over. Jordan backed himself and his natural ability and it's what separated him from others who competed against him.

Less Grip, More Flow

In our workplaces, we can become people who work in the shadow of performance-crippling fears: fear of failing, fear of damage to our reputation or standing, fear of losing money or of getting fired, fear of being overlooked for promotion or overtaken by a colleague, fear of being misunderstood, or criticized or of receiving a poor end of year rating. Fear of the worst, that so far hasn't happened. Fear can cloud our judgements, skew our perspectives and mean we freeze mid-performance.

As we've seen, the five paradigms aren't misplaced when held in elementary school, but can be hugely destructive if we retain them as adults. In a commercial environment, they mutate from being a reasonable and logical framework to a distorted exchange of imaginary power, provoking behaviours that are rooted in fear and control. When adopted by adults, Do What You're Told, Don't Answer Back, Don't Copy, Stay Out of Trouble and Teacher Knows Best all have fear of negative consequences in their DNA. Fear of getting into some sort of trouble. Fear of the teacher. Fear of detention, or of a red pen when our work gets marked. Which becomes fear of asking questions and fear of the staff room.

School with Pay can't exist without fear being present in some way in our thinking.

How's all that fear working out for you and the people you work with? Are you performing better, making greater contributions, having a greater impact and growing as individuals?

Nerves are helpful, but Fear is crippling.

When you leave School with Pay, you leave behind the paradigms that bring fear into your workplace. There's a difference between risk, nerves, unseen perils and fear.

All the other words exist as soon as you step out of the house every morning and yet most of us find a way of managing them. Risk and perils exist in every workplace and managing our way through them is part of being human. There's a difference between navigating risks and operating from fear. A fearful driver or fearful skier can sometimes be more dangerous to those around them than someone who's competent but simply going too fast.

People who fear 'grip', while those who navigate risk 'flow'.

A top athlete, musician, politician or rock star will get nervous before a performance, or may have a performance-led fear of failure. But most of the fear I see in the corporate world isn't fear because we might just be about to break the world record or deliver a virtuoso performance … it's institutional fear, which means people lock up under pressure … and for some of us, this is choking that *really* matters.

Fear grips.

Imagine doing your job according to the five *new* paradigms and being a little more fear-less in the job you do today.

Imagine working with a little less concern for the professional fears described above or operating more freely from second-guessing, negative speculation and inaccurate mind-reading.

Imagine what your professional life would be like if you shifted your attention from the possible worst that might-maybe-could-somehow happen and concentrated on being the best version of yourself that was possible and as if all potential consequences didn't really matter.

Just think about being fear-less for a moment.

Are there any differences from that, and how you normally feel or behave at work?

Start noticing from this point forward, when you begin to think, speak, or act in any way fear-fully and consider how it's impacting your performance. It's unlikely to be making it better.

With less fear to hold you back, you can put more focus on your contribution. You can experiment. You can adventure. You can use your skills and abilities to create new possibilities.

You can appreciate and leverage the strengths of others around you, because you've stopped comparing yourselves with them, are no longer be intimidated by their presence and so have no need to compete with them.

If you practice being fear-less, you might find yourself performing a little closer to the person you promised when you nailed that job interview.

Try working fear-lessly. Try playing loose. Start welcoming the rebounds and carry on shooting.

Start today. After all, what's the worst that could happen?

Back Yourself

What do you think?

What's your view?

Tell me your opinion?

We've all sat in meetings where the views being discussed are 'filtered' through the Teachers in the room. As people speak, they glance at the boss or those of a higher grade for approval, or nod over-aggressively to signal their agreement whenever they pass a comment. Full and open discussions can be constricted by concerns over whether opinions will be seen as acceptable or opinions in line with the Teacher's. And the water-line on our Icebergs keeps on rising, ever so slowly.

Too many of us look outside ourselves for approval, agreement or permission for the things we're thinking and yet if we reflect on our experience and all we've got to offer, it's often unnecessary.

Take a look the Key Experiences in Figure 3. It's a simple exercise to remind yourself of all the things you've learned and the value of your life experiences. Showing Up means carrying these around with us rather than relegating them to memories.

The start point of the exercise can be a moment in your life of your choosing, although when you started work or left school

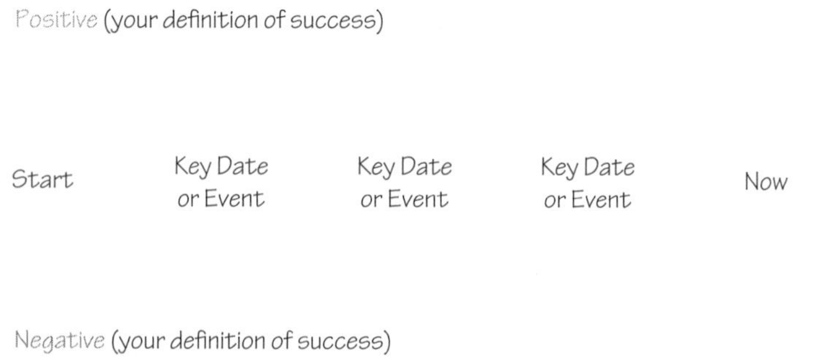

Positive (your definition of success)

	Key Date or Event	Key Date or Event	Key Date or Event	
Start				Now

Negative (your definition of success)

Figure 3: Key Experiences

for your first job is normally a good one. The end point of the exercise is Today. Your job is to mark out the key moments in your life between each of the two points: your first promotion, when you moved house, a significant job move or an event in your personal life.

The space above and below the line signifies the impact of those key moments in your life and whether they were positive or negative in terms of their impact on you. Starting from the very beginning of your career and at each key moment you've recalled, mark a spot above or below the line to reflect its impact. When you've finished, draw a line from the start of your career to each of the key impact points, connecting each one until you arrive at the present day.

Most of our lives look like a heart monitor reading – have a look at Figure 4.

Now here's the important bit: at each of the significant life/career moments that you've identified, note down two or three of the

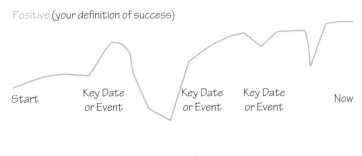

Figure 4: Life-line

key things you learned through that experience (now have a look at Figure 5). These will be a number of things:

- Patience
- Understanding
- Discipline
- Decision-Making
- Resilience
- Independence
- Inner Strength
- Determination.

When you've finished, take a look back at all the lessons you've learnt in your life; the skills you've acquired and competencies you've developed through the varied and multiple experiences you've had. It will be a long and expansive list.

Now think about today's challenges, your working environment and the professional circumstances you're currently engaged in.

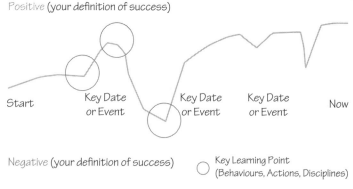

Figure 5: Learning Points

Consider the breadth and depth of your life experiences and how the things you've learned can and will help you today, in the here and now and in the things you know are coming.

You probably have more resources than you thought you had.

Remember the Believe paradigm? Backing Yourself includes remembering, owning and utilizing all the lessons you've learned and the skills and experience you've acquired through your working lifetime.

Some circumstances have been fantastic; you got promoted, were in a job you loved and everything you did seemed to be working.

Some were more challenging; a professional setback, working relationships that were difficult or a company that didn't suit you.

Simply recalling the circumstances is just to pull forward a memory, whereas reviewing those circumstances to remind yourself of what you learned, the ways you grew and how your experiences have contributed to the person you've become will give you confidence moving forward. They'll push your shoulders back and cause the fire in your eyes to intensify.

Think of all you've learned.

Back yourself rather than waiting for others to give you permission. If you wait to be asked, it might never happen, whereas to remember and integrate the breadth of your own learning is to Show Up in your fullness and allow all of us to benefit.

As we've said here already, **you have value**. You've learnt lessons that can help others, had experiences we can benefit from and your development is relevant in the work you're doing today.

Don't leave your key moments as dusty memories, filed away in the far reaches of your working story. Pull them forward, use them today, show them to the world and back yourself in the process.

You don't need to glance at Teacher when you express your next opinion. And everyone benefits from that more powerful version of you.

Break the Teacher's Mindset – lead without authority

The principal at my high school was called Mr Wills and he wore a cape to assembly. Yes, a cape.

I remember the first time he wore it, because we thought it was probably a joke. We quickly realized it wasn't. We eventually got used to Mr Wills reminding us at the start of assembly that his teacher's cape gave him authority; that it was a sign of his academic achievement and a symbol of his leadership in this part of the community.

Mr Wills' cape 'gave him authority'. Really?

One of my earliest jobs was as a project manager in the business support division of a large insurance company, finding ways to improve the performance of a function or department to make savings or reduce headcount. The 'people' I dealt with were numbers on a spreadsheet; they were a rounding error or a seasonal adjustment and there were never any faces to sit alongside any of my data. I probably wasn't great fun at a party.

And then, as mentioned earlier, I became a youth worker. I'd been volunteering at the local youth centre for a couple of years and with some local backing, a small group of us launched an ambitious new project of our own. Tribe became a career break that would last just over four years and change me forever.

At the insurance company, School with Pay was firmly installed in our corporate thinking. Hierarchy was everything and authority was the name of the game. If I asked someone 'below me' in a project team to do something, they'd do it and if my boss requested action, I'd jump equally quickly. The Teachers were in charge and the pupils were listening. But as a youth worker, I was a *nobody*. My name, rank and serial number meant nothing on a street corner and when I first started, no-one even knew my name. *'I'm Tim and I'm your local Youth Worker'* doesn't carry much weight when you ask a group of lads to stop fighting, encourage someone to quit drugs or try to stop a cycle of abusive behaviour.

I had to find new ways to communicate and an entirely new approach to making things happen. I had to Lead without Authority, because in this job, I would have none. And it meant giving priority to the first not the third word of that phrase.

In a new environment, I needed to find a way of communicating a compelling enough vision of the future that the people I was working with would decide for themselves that they would follow; as their decision and in their own way and timeframe. This was about passion and purpose and had nothing to do with position and power. I led from my energy, underpinned by my beliefs, trying to create a sense of fun and adventure in the programmes and workshops we developed for schools and local youth groups. I tried to give people a reason to follow my ideas, with a picture of the future that was about possibility and for a life that was going somewhere, rather than trying to enforce an adult-managed framework that would be instantly rejected. Tribe marked a fast-paced few years, with an amazing group of young people, many of who I'm still in touch with, some now married and with children of their own. They remembered my name eventually.

When I returned to a different division of the company I'd left four years later, I found that my style and approach to management had fundamentally changed. I still Led without Authority even though I now actually had some. And the more authority I had, the less I felt the need to use it. And this approach seemed to work, both for me and the people I was now leading.

Making a distinction between Leadership and Authority can be transformational. Without authority, all you're left with are ideas and passion. If you're a Leader without Authority, *who* you are is irrelevant; it's *what* you're about that matters. Authority is contextual and the way leaders behave in the places where they have none can be quite revealing. Even CEOs have to queue for petrol or take their place in a coffee queue and we've all worked for people who've felt the need to regularly remind us of their job title, or who assess the 'value' of the meeting they've been invited to by the other attendees' positions in the current organization chart. There are some managers who, if you took away their authority, position and structural grading would have very little to offer.

Job titles don't make you a leader and real leaders don't need them. A Leader without Authority doesn't need organizational position or grading seniority to validate their opinions or contribution. They step out from behind their job title and start *being* the activity it describes. They create other reasons for people to follow than simply because they're the Teacher, moving outside a hierarchical framework to a place focused on outcomes rather than the ins and outs of office politics.

People follow Leaders without Authority because they want to, not because they've been told to. And people who follow that sort of leader will probably run through brick walls for them.

So it's not about the cape. Leadership is revealed through actions, not assumed in an outfit or job title.

Lead without Authority. It's Adventure not Authority. It's Passion not Power.

- How would you lead, if none of your team *had* to follow you?
- How would you communicate, if people could walk out the room if they were bored or disagreed with what you were saying?
- How would you run your team or operation, if people could decide for themselves whether to turn up or not?

Tips for Leading without Authority

Talk purpose not position

Stop using your job title. Don't remind us how important you are. Show us *why* we should follow you and give us a reason to believe in you. If someone asks, describe what you're trying to achieve through the work that you do (also a good test to check that you know). When you're done, ask yourself how inspired you are by the words you've spoken, because if you're not, don't expect others to be.

Define what you do and the reason(s) why it makes a difference in the world. People follow purpose, so unless you're the President of the United States, don't rely on your position.

Ask questions

Many leaders think they have to have all the answers, ride around on a white horse and speak in a deep, booming voice to their people. You don't. If you're leading, your voice is far less valuable than your ears. When we know your ears have been working, we're more likely to tune our own pair into the words you're saying.

Ask questions. Of everyone. Ask others what they think.

Understand what your people are feeling about stuff. If you can do that and give time before responding, when you *do* speak, they'll hang on your every word.

Less I, more we

Do an I/We audit of your own language, or ask someone to do it for you. Your words will tell us where your attention is, and if you say 'I' more than you say We, you've probably got a problem.

Start flipping it round, and see how it works for you. Saying 'we' reminds us of *our* journey, that we're in this together and that there's meaning for all of us. 'We' says we're all invited to the party and that no-one'll be left unpicked in the playground in this particular game.

Enjoy the ride

If it isn't fun, it won't be followed. Lighten up a bit, and smile a little more often.

Find a way to laugh and get others laughing around you. We're much more likely to travel with you if we think we'll enjoy ourselves. Stop the bus every now and then, and let everyone out to run about or kick a football around for 20 minutes.

Waste time once in a while. It'll do wonders for your energy and you'll see it in your people.

Focus on the end-game

Know your end goal and remind people of it. **All the time.** Take people with you. Say what you're certain of and explain when you don't know, but whatever you do, **Never Stop Communicating.**

Every now and then, ask your people what they think they're working towards and check you're all still on the right track. Everyone in your team should know their purpose and if they don't, do the hard miles to get them there. The journey's pretty pointless if you get there on your own.

People who Lead without Authority have Presence. They don't hide behind their business cards, they don't use their office door as a barrier or get themselves de-railed by disputes about territory and jurisdiction. They don't need a position to convince you of their argument or slam their authority on the table to trump any hand you might be playing.

They don't need to sit at the end of the boardroom.

They don't need a desk just slightly detached from the rest of us.

They don't need the final word in every meeting.

They don't need to remind anyone that they're the boss.

They don't need a structure chart to reassure them that they're valuable.

They don't need to be Teacher and so aren't looking for any students.

The Leaver's Mindset

There's no failure, only feedback, so be fearless, back yourself and if you're a leader, lay down your authority.

Who knows what you could achieve when you're dialled in that way?

When you're operating with this updated mindset, you're primed for success and not fearful of failure. You'll stop giving power to the people, structures and circumstances around you. Your Leaver's Mindset means you've stepped out from behind outdated and fearful working paradigms and stopped playing the games that obstruct your best performance. Your setbacks are stepping stones; when in doubt you keep trying, and your passion and energy will cause people to follow, even if they don't have to. You'll continue to work hard, but now you'll work *free*, and along the way, might catch yourself smiling … because 'working' like this doesn't feel like it's work anymore …

To you there's no Failure, just plenty of Feedback. You don't see it as choking, it's critical and performance-improving learning …

…so you can afford to be fearless, because being fearful isn't effective, so you'll stare down the darkness and shoot the ball anyway …

…and by bringing to mind the wealth and breadth of your experiences and by Backing Yourself to apply them in the moment, you carry them as a toolkit and make them available to the rest of us …

…and you 'lead without authority', because inspirational people don't need a position.

Nice work. You've started Showing Up.

Now to build a plan and to get ready for some action …

GEAR 2 – YOUR OUTCOMES

All Men Dream, But not Equally

*Research on leadership by the American Management Association
has shown that the most important competency for a leader is the
ability to develop strategy. Unfortunately, when researchers
examined leaders at all levels in organizations, they found
only 4% to be strategists.*
Rich Horwath, Deep Dive, Greenleaf Book Group, 2009

EVERY leader? The *most* important competency? Only 4 percent?
Really? Why?

*All men dream, but not equally. Those that dream by night in the
dusty recesses of their minds, wake in the day to find that it
was vanity; but the dreamers of the day are dangerous men, for
they may act out their dreams with open eyes,
to make them happen.*
T.E. Lawrence (Lawrence of Arabia)

I'm not sure it's about Strategy, or the 4 percent who might be
talented in it. I think it's about when we have our *dreams* and
what we do to make them a reality.

'All men dream ...' is a stunning quote and its insight is piercing.

How many people do you know who've described an idea, imagined a goal or expressed a desire to make something happen and are still saying the same things many years later, having taken no action or responsibility to make it happen? The world is full of people who have ideas without plans, dreams without commitment and aspirations without execution.

Have you got a vision for yourself *today* that is so compelling that it influences the way you live, moment by moment and day by day?

Or is it just a dream?

You see, dreaming is easy. We don't have to take responsibility for the 'dusty recesses of our minds' while we're snoozing in our armchairs, allowing our minds to wander in adventures that are impossible and which require no accountability. We can be a fireman or a superhero and have breath-taking adventures, only to realize when we wake that life's still normal, with the same routine, the same circumstances and in entirely unchanged, all-familiar surroundings. **Dreams on their own have no power to change anything.** They're all over once the morning comes and we return to a reality where nothing much has changed – we can't really fly, we didn't save the world, we didn't really win gold at the Olympics and the most gorgeous people in the world aren't really our partners (yet).

Dreaming by night is soon-dusty memory, full of ideas without action, in adventures that are shown to ultimately be vanity – an altered version of ourselves without any base in reality.

But dreaming when you're *awake*? Well that changes *everything*.

Dreamers of the day truly *are* dangerous people, because they walk out their dreams and step into their reality. Their sleep is for rest, not to reflect on what could have, would have, should have or might have been. Their dreams might become reality, and it's this fact alone that makes them wonderfully dangerous.

- How many of your dreams are alive in your day today, and what **right now**, are you doing to make them a reality?
- How many of your plans are dusty and unactioned, destined to dissolve as soon as the sun leaks though the curtains and your alarm gets you up for another day in the classroom?

But hold on. Don't feel too bad. When were we *ever* taught to dream in the day? Which one of the five old paradigms trained us to think about our outcomes, to create a personal plan or to set ourselves a target?

Answer = None. Just do what you're told. The Teacher knows best, so don't bother answering back to them. Concentrate on your own work and don't ever get in any trouble.

When we were children, Teacher held our hand as we crossed the road. We were handed a kit list before going on a school trip. Revision guides, past papers, step-by-step instructions and painting by numbers. All perfect for children yet, as we've seen, entirely growth-stunting for adults.

Eventually, we have to walk across main roads for ourselves. But when active in our job titles, our to-do lists and our objectives, School with Pay thinking leaves us silently grasping for the hand of someone 'bigger' than ourselves. Someone who'll watch out for us, have our back or hear our unexpressed dreams and turn them into reality.

And we wonder why so many of us can't think for ourselves any more. Here's a way to plan with our five new paradigms running:

Well-Formed Outcomes

Effective outcome thinking is an essential skill and a muscle that needs stretching, yet too often finds itself at the bottom of our ever-growing action list or continually postponed until the pattern becomes clearer ... and our days become the weeks become the months become the years of our lives, without us ever taking a seat at the controls of our own activity. We hurtle through life and rarely stop to ask some simple questions – how did we get here and where do we want to go next?

But let's scale back from life plans and big picture thinking for a moment – how many of us even know what we want at a most basic level; for our lives, our families and our futures?

The truth is, many of us know in detail what we *don't* want, but far less of us have clarity on precisely what we *do* want. We might want to change our jobs or our career, our house, our image or even our partners but often don't have any clarity on exactly what those changes need to be. Things need to be different, we just don't know how, or why ... or when. Faced with too many options (all of which seem attractive compared with our current situation), we can find ourselves bouncing from plan to plan, person to person and job to job, all in a vain search to find the one thing that we haven't made the effort to define clearly ... we just know ... or hope ... or guess ... that we'll know what it is once when we get there ... won't we?

Many of our dreams, hopes and outcomes are badly formed and this can be for a number of reasons – we may not know what we really want, what we're after may not be in our control or we may lack the time, finances, support or any number of important resources in order to make them happen. And if our thinking is problem focused rather than outcome focused, our attention is on the problem, not the solution, and just like a skier, where our attention is will determine where we go.

If your plans aren't well-formed, they won't be 'well likely' to succeed or deliver the results you're after. Too often, we allow the voices in our head to trick us into thinking that our ideas and dreams are clear and robust and we can easily start blaming other people when our circumstances don't match what we expected or when we don't end up getting what we want.

In my experience, SMART objectives (Specific, Measurable, Achievable, Realistic, Timely) only get us so far.

SMART is a great model, it's just that objectives built that way don't seem very effective at igniting our passion. Whilst working with the acronym brings clarity and measurement to our plans, when have you ever discussed them energetically with friends at a dinner party or framed them in the bathroom to review as you got ready every morning? Even the word 'objective' is pretty boring if we're honest, and seems devoid of personality. It's fine for a sales target, a performance metric or another kind of number, but not when it's about *us*, our lives and our futures.

I want to take us beyond objective-setting, to life-transformational **Well-Formed Outcome Thinking**. This isn't new thinking and it certainly isn't my design – if you Google the phrase today, you'll find many resources that will help you. Developing well-formed outcomes is the second of our four components and offers a powerful method of structured thinking to help you to frame, to plan, to walk into your goals and to consistently get more of what you want more often.

We all have responsibilities and things that we're 'on the hook' for, but outcome thinking points us to something more powerful and to something outside of ourselves; it points us to Purpose.

When our work has purpose for us, our personal contribution becomes critical and too important to leave to chance. Purpose gets us up in the morning. Purpose gives us meaning. People with well-formed outcomes are the dangerous men and women that T.E. Lawrence was referring to.

Well-formed outcomes take your thinking somewhere deeper, to the point of *really* knowing what you **really** want (for real) and then identifying the targeted actions you need to take in order to make the dream happen. It was transformational when I was introduced to it many years ago and I still use its principles on a professional and personal level. Well-formed outcome thinking uses just six key questions and an invitation at the end.

The Outcome Wheel (see Figure 6) is a quick way to review the six questions and do the thinking that's necessary before you take

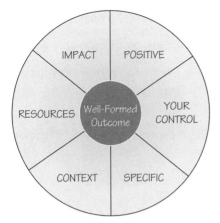

Positive - What do you (really) want?

Control - Can you initiate and do it?

Specific - What and how?

Context - Where, when, with whom?

Resources - What do you need that you don't already have?

Impact - What are the consequences (on people and things)? Is that OK?

Figure 6: Outcome Wheel

action. The questions will probe whether your outcome is well-formed or even if it's your real outcome.

1. Get positive

What do you *really* want? Ask this question a few times and you'll always get closer to the real answer. Outcome thinking focuses on the goals that are ahead of you, not the present states or situations that you want to leave behind, which describe a problem-based mindset.

Are you heading towards something or away from it? Language is important here and yours will tell you where your attention and focus is. **Stay in the positive.** Look at the list below and notice the different energy and emphasis when an outcome points *towards* something, rather than negative and *away* from it:

I want to lose weight	I want to be fit
I don't want to have another argument	I want to achieve agreement

I want to give up smoking	I want to be healthy
I want less stress	I want to be relaxed
I don't want to work here	I want to work somewhere that ...

If your current thinking is problem-centred, try asking 'What do I *really* want instead of that ...?'

2. Keep it in your control

Does your outcome rely solely on you (see below)? Are you the person who can instigate the activity? Are you the one who can make it happen?

OUTSIDE YOUR CONTROL	WELL-FORMED
To win the race	To maximize my training
To be promoted	To be an example of professionalism
To get a pay rise	To meet well-defined performance goals
To make my children happy	To be a caring, understanding and guiding parent
To be the next Prime Minister	To learn about getting into politics

If you can't control it, you're outcome isn't well-formed.

If it's not well-formed, it's unlikely you'll achieve it. Let it go and adjust it to one that you CAN deliver and that you do have the power to make happen.

3. Get specific

Drill down to a level of clarity for your outcome so that you know how to describe it in detail:

What will be the evidence that your outcome's been achieved?

How will you know when you've got there?

What's going on around you and what are you doing? What will you see, hear and feel when you've got it?

4. Check the context

Turn the clock forward to a time and context when you have your outcome in full.

Where will you have your outcome?

When will you have your outcome?

How will you be experiencing it?

5. Check your resources

What resources do you already have?

What resources do you need, that you don't already have?

The resources you need might be multiple: time, money, knowledge, understanding, capacity, support etc. and you might even find yourself walking back through this wheel to develop a well-formed outcome for acquiring the resource(s) you need.

A top tip that I've also found useful when looking at resources is to draw on past experiences and apply their learning and principles to your current outcome. What evidence might you have of achieving something like this before?

As an example, if your outcome is to acquire a new skill, do you drive a car? If you do, well, very few people are born as babies able to competently drive a motor vehicle, so if you can drive today, you have a previous and personal reference point for successfully learning a skill that at one time you had no understanding of or competency in.

What might be useful for you to remember about *that* process that you can apply to this new learning?

Now that we've established you have the capacity to learn a skill from scratch, how can you use those experiences to back your ability in the process now ahead of you?

6. Check the impact

What do you stand to gain if you have your outcome?

What do you stand to lose if you have it?

What impact will your outcome have on the key people and things around you? Is that OK?

* * *

Can you see how these six steps bring structure to your thinking and enable you to identify your first step in making your outcome happen?

One final question might push this a step further:

If you acted *now* as if you'd already achieved your outcome, how might your behaviour *today* be different? What stops you adopting that behaviour immediately, by living your dream and walking into its reality?

You might be surprised by your answer and could already have your first step ...

Which bit bites you?

In my experience of working with this model over a number of years, a few people regularly trip up over one or two specific aspects of the model and find other aspects far more straight-forward. Some questions seem to bite us in the backside and updating those patterns in our thinking can have a profound effect.

Here are some examples from my own life and experience that bring (well-formed) outcomes to life and show the six questions in action:

At the end of 2002, as a 31-year-old husband and father, I accepted a late night and beer-soaked New Year's Eve challenge from a close friend to run the New York Marathon the following November. I hadn't run for more than three miles in any direction at any time of any year. It was an amazing journey. Finishing my first marathon in Central Park in 2003 was one of the most memo-rable experiences of my life at that point, in what quickly became my clear favourite city in the world. I was hooked.

Being a goal-orientated person and enjoying a fitness challenge, I promptly set myself the target of running five marathons in total before I was 40, with two of the remaining four to be again run in New York.

Congratulations me. Very impressive.

Off I went, diving into training and learning about running, buying any magazine with a running shoe on the cover and sharing stories (which meant comparing times) with other runners and marathon veterans wherever I could find them. And in 2005 I was back in New York ticking off marathon number 2.

The Outcome Wheel was brilliant for my training and helped me set realistic goals, focus on what I could control and run with a wonderfully clear mindset. Or so I thought.

In the summer of 2007, I started training for marathon number 3, to be my third in that favourite city and a key element of my '5 by 40' outcome. Nice one. I was also working in Central London, had a fulfilling yet busy job with a 4-hour total commute every day, a wife and growing family back home and two sets of parents living in the local area. I'd missed a few parents' evenings (the real ones) and most of the kids' school productions. I didn't see my wife much and was working in the week and running at weekends. Oh, and I'd forgotten about my parents and in-laws. But not to worry, I was nailing my running outcome.

Eventually, Steph, Jack and Lucy sat me down on a beautiful summer's evening and very gently and calmly explained that this 'wasn't quite working for them'.

Of course, the conversations that took place and the environment they took place in was *nothing like* I've described. No-one talked calmly, and this was far more Simpsons than Waltons. To hear, I needed something far more than 'gentle', but eventually and reluctantly, I finally got the message.

I'm an outcome junkie. And it's their *impact* that bites me.

I have no trouble with being positive, adjusting outcomes that aren't in my control and getting specific and clear on the context and resources. My challenge is in understanding or being interested enough about the impact my outcomes have on other people and things.

I've changed jobs, moved my family, booked marathons and set directions before taking account of all the impacts those things might have on other people and things. I've achieved most of the many goals I've set in my life, but some left collateral damage that might have been unnecessary if I hadn't skipped the 6th question and jumped straight to action. Or stopped using 'I' or 'Me' quite as much and chosen the odd 'Us' (only ever occasionally).

My wife and kids had a point ... kind of ... maybe. I eventually adjusted my schedule, involved them in my outcome and we found a way to still achieve 5 by 40 but with their needs and desires included and without it having such an impact on them. It was important learning, which they'd say I'm still working on!

I ran my 5th marathon in Berlin in 2010, aged 38. It wasn't about giving up the dream, but it was about doing it differently. It was about asking *all six* questions. And having a patient family.

A couple of other examples of outcome thinking in action:

I once chatted through the Outcome Wheel with a client with two teenage sons, who wanted to organize a lads' outdoor adventure weekend, focused around canoeing in his favourite Loire Valley. One of his sons was fully on board, while the other wasn't interested, which was leaving Dad frustrated and disappointed that the trip hadn't yet been finalized.

We didn't even get past the first two questions. Far from being 'to take my boys away for the weekend', what my client *really* wanted was for his eldest son to want to do what Dad wanted to do, in a place where Dad wanted to do it and have the same level of excitement about the prospect that Dad and number 2 son were experiencing.

Other people's feelings aren't in your control.

When Dad realized what he'd been really going for, it all made perfect sense, and we ditched his badly-formed outcome in order to generate a well-formed one.

Heading back to question 1, his outcome was updated, because what my client really, really wanted was 'to spend some quality time with my boys', which prompted a whole series of questions for them to discuss as a trio and discover what 'quality time' could look like for all three of them. Canoeing in France might happen in another way, but as another separate outcome with six new questions of its own. His priority right now was time with the boys, and once they'd discussed it, the activity could be anything.

Another client had an outcome to swim the English Channel, but hadn't ever thought about when and had been talking about it for years (Specific). Why is it that the timeframe for so many of our undelivered goals is 'a couple of years', as though it's the magic number? This client had been talking about this *dream* for almost ten now, and it was gathering dust and only emerged when he was sleeping.

Not so long ago, someone in a workshop said they'd 'always really wanted' to learn to play the guitar and thought they'd probably have a talent for it.

They hadn't got round to buying a guitar yet (Resources).

In my experience, Well-Formed Outcome Thinking takes us beyond SMART objectives to the things that for us are truly meaningful; to goals that generate passion, utilize our strengths and that we'd talk about at a party. Well-Formed Outcomes get you involved, they get you invested and can normally get you moving.

Imagine if your working objectives and goals were more than just an acronym and got you excited and out of bed in the morning?

Today, if your work objectives are in a drawer or you can't immediately recall them, pull them out and update them. **Fast.** Brush the dust off and make them alive while you're awake.

Don't waste any more time on objectives you're not invested in. If necessary, do business with your stakeholders to re-work them into something more meaningful. Or if you don't need the hassle, sit quiet in the school lesson. Maybe, eventually, Teacher will give the answer.

All men dream, but not equally.

What do **you** really want?

GEAR 3 – YOUR STRENGTHS

Focus on Strengths

Everyone is talented. You're talented. I'm talented.

But do you believe it?

Can you say 'I'm talented', to yourself, without giggling, brushing it off or looking around to see if anyone heard you?

You *are* talented.

And you told us you were. Remember that interview? How many of us got the jobs we're doing by describing how utterly talentless, useless and unhelpful to a business we would be? In our interviews, we talked about what we could do and gave an insight into those areas in which we were (moderately, if we're British) talented. And that's what our employer bought ... and therefore what they're rightfully expecting.

A strengths-based operating philosophy, a focus on strengths or on strengths-based leadership, is nothing new. Dr Donald Clifton was a leadership researcher and expert on Strengths Psychology, who, with Gallup in the 1960s, conducted over 20,000 near-identical 90-minute interviews with leaders across multiple sectors, industries and backgrounds, alongside gathering their individual performance data. From this solid research foundation, his team reviewed the traits and competencies at play in defining leadership performance. Their results and conclusions were not as they'd expected.

Far from identifying a few key strengths that were shared by all the best leaders, Clifton discovered something else, and speaking in 2003 said:

> *What great leaders have in common is that each truly knows his or her strengths and can call on the right strength at the right time. This explains why there is no definitive list of characteristics that describe all leaders.*

In the 1990s, the Clifton Strengthsfinder online tool was developed and has evolved and been improved over time. It's a tool that we regularly recommend and work with in our consultancy practice. These days, there are a number of other strengths-based tools out there, although for me, the impact of Strengthsfinder's 34 signature talent themes and the ongoing results with our client teams and individuals continue to be compelling.

Almost 10 million people will have completed one of Gallup's strengths assessment tools by the end of 2013. Like any profiling tool you might have come across or experienced, it's probably not perfect, but judging by its results, I really like it.

The headline output from Gallup's research builds a compelling case for individuals and organizations to adopt a strengths-based approach to leadership and their team operations, growth and development:

- Only 20 percent of people when asked said that they had the chance to play to their strengths most of the time while they were working, which is like being in a job where for four out of every five days you did work that didn't allow you to operate at your best.
- Only 25 percent of people surveyed discussed strengths during their performance reviews, which means that a massive 75 percent of performance reviews must be focused on weaknesses. This must be the equivalent of being a human punch bag for an hour every month or a bit longer each quarter.
- People and organizations that focus on strengths were 50 percent more likely to have lower employee turnover, 38 percent more likely to be more productive as teams and 44 percent more likely to deliver high customer satisfaction.
- And finally, people who develop their strengths are statistically more likely to have more fun at a party (*I added the last one*).

Focusing on strengths might be an approach and philosophy that's finally of its time. I've never known a period where a strengths-based approach to leadership and performance has resonated more with teams and individuals and so it maybe should come as no surprise that in 2013 Gallup began to adopt a far more open approach to its training, coaching and strengths-learning resources, declaring a vision to see one billion people across the world understanding their personal strengths, supported by a million coaches to help them leverage the benefits.

Focusing on strengths Works.

I've never had a conversation with someone to review and discuss their strengths where they didn't break into a smile at some point, and occasionally those conversations have unlocked far more emotion. Focusing on strengths feels instinctively right for many of us, although it can often seem counter-cultural in a world of performance management processes, competency frameworks and forced performance distribution curves (Hall Monitor, anyone?).

I like the profiling tools, but not as much as I *love* the philosophy.

We *all* have strengths and areas where we're talented. We *all* have gifts and abilities and things to offer any team, if we're switched on, alive and ready to make a difference.

What if we all took our talents seriously enough to strive to become better at the things we're already pretty gifted at?

How many of our performance review discussions start by covering a few of the things that have gone well over the period and then focus on development areas and end with people signing up for courses and writing personal development plans focused on making them more well-rounded or broadening their skill-set. Makes sense in principal. But how many people do you know or have heard about who achieved something ground-breaking, remarkable, paradigm-shifting and history-making who were also fully rounded and wholly balanced human beings?

History is often made by people who are somewhat less than balanced. 'Well-rounded' is a myth and could be the corporate equivalent of grey, vanilla, standard or average.

Mo Farah is the British long and middle distance runner, who followed up incredible performances to win 5000 and 10,000 metres gold at the London 2012 Olympics with wins in both disciplines at the 2013 World Championships, becoming only the second man in history to win double-gold alongside Ethiopia's Kenenisa Bekele (in 2008/2009).

Ground-breaking performance. Breakthrough. History-making.

If Mo was in one of our performance review meetings, we'd probably suggest he have a go at the javelin.

Mo Farah isn't a perfectly well-rounded athlete. I'm not sure he'd be great in the scrum at rugby. What he *is* though, is *awesome* at what he is good at and he trains relentlessly and daily to become 0.25 percent, 0.50 percent or 1 percent better … at **the things he's already incredibly talented at**.

Steve Jobs practised for many, many hours, weeks before his famous keynote addresses to launch new Apple products. He was already good at presenting, some would say great. But he practised. Relentlessly.

Much has been written about the 10,000 hours principle for skills development researched by psychologist Dr K. Anders Ericsson, which was popularized by Malcolm Gladwell in his book *Outliers*, published in 2008. The same principle can be applied to developing the behavioural characteristics you're already naturally gifted in. We all have abilities … and if we trained them past 10,000 hours, who knows what we could achieve with them?

Gallup say that Talent x Investment = Strength. You are Talented. And when you're intentional and focused on investing in those talents, the strengths that emerge might just be remarkable.

This, for me, is real Performance Management.

It's not just about templates, competencies and standard frameworks. It's about understanding your talents, getting your head in good order and applying them purposefully to outcomes that are well-formed and which can leverage them. Now *that* would be a good weekly schedule to work to.

Who Needs Balance?

Focusing on strengths is not about becoming 'balanced'. As we've already seen, when All is Well, who needs balance?

I want my books to be balanced.

I want my airplane to be well-balanced.

I want my diet to be (reasonably) well-balanced.

I don't want my performance to be balanced. I want work that stretches, trains and leverages the things I'm already good at and have the potential to be outstanding in. I want my work life to be lung-busting, leg-breaking, heart-rushing, off the charts, impossible to catch and kinda scary.

Why shouldn't our professional lives feel like that? We spend too many hours each day in them to allow them to be balanced, or medium or average.

Have you ever felt dizzy after a performance review, because your manager was coaching and pushing you to take your natural talents and stretch them beyond what you even imagined was possible ... or did you just get a 'rating' and sent on an influencing or assertiveness course?

I'm not knocking development or courses that may help us, but I am knocking a drive for well-roundedness. Performance can and should be focused on *the remarkable* and the evidence suggests that raising awareness and then intentionally focusing on strengths delivers a greater return than majoring on the opposite. And my experience with clients and colleagues backs this up.

Switching our minds to focusing on strengths rather than poring over and majoring on areas of weakness requires a new language to be spoken by us as individuals, the people who manage us and the organizations we're part of. Being intentional about developing what we *are* rather than what we're not might be a new way for you to operate, but if you give it time, I'm convinced you'll find it pays dividends.

It will also enable you to break forever the Don't Copy paradigm. When we discover as individuals what we're naturally good at and are encouraged to push those things further in terms of our performance, we become more aware of the gifts and talents of others and the ways in which we can collaborate to maximize our overall impact. Imagine working in a national network and knowing you can call up your counterparts from the four corners of the country to leverage their talents, instincts and approaches to the challenges you find yourself facing, rather than struggling alone, trying to cover all the bases. If we're not well-rounded, but gifted in certain areas … we *have* to copy and it might just help every one of us perform better.

I could write more on Strengths or Leading from Strengths, but I'd rather you hear it direct from the guys who literally wrote the book(s) on it. Although there are others, I'd recommend jumping online and grabbing one of Gallup's Strengthsfinder books or reading more about the tool by visiting www .gallupstrengthscenter.com. Take the test, discover your strengths and read through their suggested actions. Even better would be to initiate a supporting conversation with a Strengths coach, to help you adjust to what might be a new way of thinking.

Think Strengths.

Think Differently.

GEAR 4 – YOUR TIME

It's All in Your Schedule

Mindset. Outcomes. Strengths.

If School with Pay is rooted in fear and transfers personal power to others around us, a **mindset** that contains five new paradigms helps retain our personal power and manage any ongoing mind tricks that might invite us to regress to those childlike ways of working.

Developing **outcomes** that are well-formed focuses our efforts on the things we can control, with specific and effective plans that deliver what we really want (as well as managing the impact of us having them!)

Discovering our talents reaffirms our natural and hard-wired abilities, taking them seriously enough for us to apply effort and energy in seeing them owned, understood, developed and leveraged as **strengths** in the work we get paid for.

When you strengthen your mindset, nail your outcomes and invest in your strengths, you'll find yourself more aware of all the possibilities your giftings create and the impact they can have in the world around you. And as you step out from behind the five old paradigms, it's time to review your schedule and the various ways in which you're managing the **time** you have.

Until you value yourself, you won't value your time.
Until you value your time, you won't do anything with it.
M. Scott Peck

Have you ever reached the end of your day and said 'I don't know where the time's gone today ...'?

Time. It's the thing some of us need most and yet often seems the scarcest. I don't meet many working people who've got time on their hands. We're time-poor and wear it like a badge to justify our existence.

'How are you?'

'Good, good. **BUSY!**'

'Not bad thanks. **BUSY.**'

'Okaaay. Pretty **FULL ON** at the moment.'

It's as though we add the second phrase as justification that we're human; as though if we didn't say we were busy or add a rider to our answer our commitment would be doubted or our effort brought into question.

Stand up. Teacher's behind you, and as ever, they're listening.

Where your attention is, is where you'll go. What you tell yourself will grow. What would it take for you to answer a different way?

'How are you?'

'I'm really **happy.**'

'Great. **Learning** loads.'

'Alright thanks. **Thinking clearly.** How are you getting on?'

Alongside getting you a few strange looks, these different answers could be like shoving a stick in the front wheel of your mindset's speeding bicycle. They stop your hamster wheel. They're the mental 'tilt' for your pinball machine. And you probably need it.

Everyone's busy. That's not impressive. Even ants are busy.

I'm more interested in what we're all busy Doing or Creating or Impacting or Becoming than simply how hard we're working, how long our action lists are or how may emails we're getting in every day that our worlds keep on spinning (OK, you win, you can be the email Prom Queen and yes, you're very important, yes, you're incredibly popular and yes, I'm sure we *are* all mightily impressed etc. etc.).

I was talking to a client just recently who answered my 'How are you?' with '*It's pretty full-on*', before realizing who he was speaking to and what I'd probably ask next. He paused, before saying, 'OK, what do I mean by that, why did I answer that way?' In a few short sentences he articulated in detail what he was *really* thinking, his current reactions and also a few plans and options for improvements. By describing it out loud to an audience, he reminded himself of where his head was at, and what was really going on in his full-on environment and most importantly how his mindset might be affecting his performance.

I'm not sure I even said anything.

Busy is Easy. Design takes Effort. Intentional time management takes action, graft and attention and the state of your schedule today will reveal many of the paradigms you're working from.

Try *not* saying you're busy now and then. Find other words to describe your existence. Notice your internal reactions as well as those around you. If you could do with establishing a better relationship with the time you don't have, Updates to those words will always be Available.

In school we were given our timetable. Our pre-arranged schedule of where to be, at what time and which books we'd need to bring with us. Double period maths on a Friday. Never enough sports lessons. And of course, if we're running a School with Pay mindset, it's just possible we're taking no more responsibility for our schedules than we did our school timetables. How much of our language when we talk about our time management and diaries has a 'done to' feel to it, deflects personal responsibility and pretends we have no options? You've got French on a Monday. Deal with it.

Leaving School means taking responsibility and what you do with the time you have will make or break your performance.

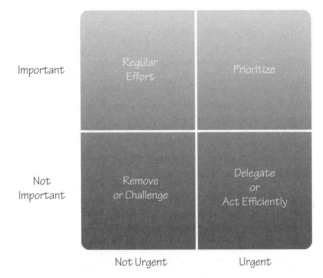

Figure 7: Where Does All Your Time Go?

Where's Your Head At?

You're probably familiar with this time management grid, which again is not my design, but which is often incredibly helpful. The idea here is that you identify and then allocate your tasks and projects into one of the four boxes and take the relevant action depending on its category (see Figure 7).

The problem is, the distortions of School with Pay thinking often contaminate what should be a useful and practical tool. Very often when I ask client teams to work with the grid and allocate their tasks to one of the four boxes, it becomes like a game of Corporate Chicken, with everyone looking at each other's answers before making a selection. Adults in short trousers busily scribble down task after task after task, occasionally looking up to check what their colleagues are writing. Spelling test anyone?

As you'd expect when everyone's a student, few people will admit that they have any responsibilities that on reflection are neither urgent or important. The whole process needs a jolt to release a bit of honesty and there are a couple of ways I think achieve this.

Before we play with those, let's look at the grid itself:

There are two simple steps:

1. Write down a numbered list of your headline responsibilities and objectives. These are your tasks and responsibilities, objectives and projects, goals and to-do lists and any professional things you're currently on the hook for.
2. When you've captured everything, draw up the 4-box grid and allocate each task's number to one of the 4 box combinations of Urgent and/or Important. Give an honest allocation for how you're currently living, rather than what you think you should be doing or by flicking to the end of this chapter ...

If you did this properly, you'll be able to see that Scott Peck was right. When you're asked to note down your task list and allocate it across four simple boxes, you get far more data than you were probably expecting. Right in front of you, you'll have a representation of how you're 'holding' your job right now and the current patterns of your thinking. Your dominant working mindset and current working paradigms will be laid out before you on the page ... and the only question will now be whether they're really working for you. Don't believe me? Here's why ...

Most of what we say to ourselves about our schedules is **all made up**. When we pause and scratch beneath the surface, most of our daily working experience is peppered with distractions, inattention, lack of clarity, temporary focus, confusion, misunderstanding, laziness, auto-pilot thinking and leaving things to chance. And yet we still kid ourselves that our work is All Important.

Often when we complete the grid, our activity list drifts north towards the Urgent row and maybe slightly to the right (the Important column). Take a good look at the shape of your allocation. Many people convince themselves that they're running the UN or are something like Leader of the Free World, which is why all their work must be so important and not open to challenge.

You're not. It's not. It might be made up and could be nearly killing you.

Is *everything* you do Important? Is *everything* Urgent?

When *everything's* Important, nothing is. When *everything's* Urgent, nothing is.

Two things I want to do with the grid you've got in front of you:

First of all, have a read though the tasks you first listed. Sometimes our schedules are so cluttered with immediate priorities that we lose perspective on the broader purpose of the roles we're doing. It's amazing the sorts of 'tasks' that people and particularly managers 'delete' from their regular day-job lists.

I wonder if you did too? Did you allocate a category for:

- Personal development
- Thinking time
- Reading, watching or listening to industry experts or people of interest
- Researching or learning more about your sector
- Receiving coaching/mentoring
- Free time
- Seeing how my team are doing
- Time for the unexpected (see below)
- Open discussions, brainstorms or group-think sessions with no specific or 'urgent' outcome
- Spending time with people who are better at your job than you in order to learn from them
- Ringing peers to ask for advice or gather their perspective on a problem or challenge.

Did the list above make it onto your grid alongside all your other tasks?

And if not, why not? Aren't they an equally important part of your job description?

What could you do differently to make them more important to you? Oh, and before you say you 'just forgot' and that they are of course important to you, trust the process. You noted down the things that were 'front of mind' to you and the things you didn't recall give you data on where they sit in your current mindset; at the back, discarded or maybe gathering dust? And, as ever, Where your Attention is ...

The second step is to play Runaround.

Runaround

Runaround was a children's TV game show that ran in the UK between 1975 and 1981. The UK version of an American original, it was most famously hosted by UK comedian Mike Reid and involved a group of children being asked three-option multiple choice questions before running to an area of the studio marked out for their chosen answer. Of course, once each child had chosen their answer, they'd compare their choice with the other kids around them … and maybe doubt their first choice. At this point, Mike Reid would shout '**Runaraaaaaaaand – NOW!**' in his trademark London accent and each child had one chance to change their answer, before discovering if they'd made the right choice.

Questions, prizes and group dynamics. Perfect. The rest of the show was standard scoring, with the eventual winner winning something like a Scalextric (we were easily pleased, back in the day).

Runaround is a great game to play with your time management grid and even better if it's with a trusted colleague or coach who's willing to challenge your thinking. Review your grid and try and move your answers. Resist the temptation to move your tasks to the top-right of the grid and challenge yourself to move something to bottom-left. Take responsibility for your thinking and challenge your categorizations.

- Is that task *really* that important?
- Is it *really* that urgent?

- Have you *honestly* got no tasks in Not Urgent/Not Important? Does that mean you've never come out of a meeting and said '*Well that was a waste of time*' and if not, aren't you due back at The White House shortly?

A few questions to ask yourself about your list before you play Runaround:

- Is your allocation really true ... and how can you be certain?
- How closely does your grid match your current job description?
- If you'd been given your task list as you've presented it and offered it as a job, would you have accepted it? Why are you accepting it now?
- How closely does your grid represent what your boss, stakeholders, team and customers expect, want and likely need to see from you?
- How are your strengths reflected in the page in front of you and how much of your time are you spending bringing your best to the table?
- Finally, if you were to show your friends and family your grid, how confident are you that they'd look at you with pride and say 'That's work you were born for ...'?

Stretching Time

I believe we can stretch time or at least feel as though we're stretching it, because so many of us waste it and aren't even aware of it. If your head, plan and strengths are switched on and firing, what you spend your time on and the places where you're spending it becomes critical, so why are so many of us leaving it to chance?

Here are a few examples of how we can all stretch the time we have and make ourselves more effective.

Seven-minute Meetings

Why don't we have seven-minute meetings? Why is every meeting we schedule for 30 minutes, or an hour and how often do we 'put 2 hours in, just in case'.

Don't blame Outlook, blame the ways you're working.

Book a 12-minute meeting, a 19-minute update or a 26-minute discussion and then halfway through, check you've covered off 50 percent of the planned agenda. Give proper thought to the time you need to review an issue or complete a task, rather than rounding it up to the nearest half day. You can always talk faster if you have to.

Park the Politeness

Maybe I'm not a fan of small-talk, but some people seem to have turned it into a sport. How many of our 30-minute regular meetings look like this:

- Start with 10 minutes of 'warm-up', while people get settled, arrive late, chat about the weather or abuse each other on the latest sports results.
- 10 minutes of actual business gets done (because that's all the time that was really needed).
- The meeting closes with 10 minutes of 'final friendlies', while people ask about the family, update on gossip or talk in sidebar whispers to one or two of the attendees about the

things they *really* wanted to talk about but that weren't on the agenda and are the real reason they attended for the initial 20 minutes.

Build strong and effective working relationships. Know the purpose and outcomes of the work you're doing together. Establish a foundation with your team-mates, so that you can arrange a 10-minute meeting, get straight down to business and still be friends afterwards. Maybe it would also mean not having to add 'have a good weekend' to each email you send on a Friday ...

Know Your Contribution

I once sat on a steering group of a particular project in a financial services organization. We met quarterly at the company headquarters and in one of the boardrooms on the executive floor. With an attendance list of over 20 people, these were days to do governance, review papers and represent our respective divisions of the business. Personally, it meant a five-hour commute and an all-day meeting. I didn't say *anything* for the first two I attended (unusual for me), as I genuinely had nothing useful or appropriate to contribute. Two days, 10 hours of commuting, a few hundred pounds spent on train tickets and a couple of nice lunches. And I was already 'busy'.

At the start of the third meeting and before we dived into a third full agenda, I finally made my first contribution:

> *Morning everyone. Before we kick off, I just have a quick question.*
> *Can anyone tell me what my unique contribution to this*
> *meeting is? This is my 3rd meeting with you, and I'm*

conscious I haven't contributed anything in the previous two.
I'm not sure myself what I'm bringing to the table and
so with respect to everyone else here, if you can't tell me,
I'd like to excuse myself. I've travelled already and so
will just be outside, but don't want to remain here
and repeat this for a 3rd day.

Tumbleweed blew through the boardroom.

After a few seconds (which felt like an hour), the guy sat next to me said, 'I've been coming here for 6 months and I don't know what we're doing either ...'

We were finally able to pause the planned agenda and spend a valuable chunk of that day's meeting on re-establishing our purpose and redefining each person's required contribution and I eventually agreed for someone more junior but far more experienced to attend in my place going forward, which made all of us happier. The meeting didn't need seniority, it needed understanding and expertise. It needed people who were experts, not a selection of Teachers in a staff room.

Know your contribution. You don't have time to waste any train tickets.

Stop CC'ing Us, We Really Don't Care

Have you ever thought you'd like to get a few *more* emails pinging into your inbox?

Do you regularly get cc'd on emails you're not interested in?

I once worked in a company where the cc'ing of emails had become a way of life; to justify people's existence, to give 'updates' on things we didn't need to know but were being told anyway, or which released the passive-aggressive behaviour of people who'd fallen out with each other but were inviting you to watch their argument, as though having *your* name on the distribution list somehow justified their position. It was bullshit.

I had a PA at the time and we discovered the facility on my emails to set an auto-response according to specific parameters. I set a rule so that anyone cc'ing me on emails received the following reply:

> *Thanks for your message. I don't read cc'd emails. My PA, Sharon*
> *scans all of them and once a week will pass on the*
> *ones she thinks I'll be interested in. If you need me to do*
> *something specifically, can I ask that you re-email me*
> *and let me know exactly what you need and we'll take*
> *it from there. Thanks.*

I also said to Sharon that if she *ever* passed me a cc'd email, I would kill her. Brilliant.

Do the Maths

When you meet with other colleagues, consider the annual salary of everyone in the room and the collective cost to the company of the time you'll be spending together. Once you've done the maths, check that the value of the meeting's Outcome and Impact is *greater* than the sum of your equivalent planned time investment.

If it isn't, stop meeting and go to confession or improve the ways you're working. If you don't, this meeting will be *costing* you money.

When it comes to the Time you spend, start by balancing the books.

Here's a final example that shows the impact when we leave our Mindset, Outcomes, Strengths and Time to chance. It's a real story, with names changed to protect the not-so-innocent.

An insurance company I was working in was arranging a two-day company offsite for its middle-managers across the country. A small working group was arranged to own the design and delivery on behalf of the broader executive leadership team and included nine operational leaders (including me) and one executive, together with the MD of an external event management company. We would be working on behalf of a stakeholder group of almost 50 people and it was agreed that we'd be given 'full authority and accountability' to pull it all together on behalf of the broader group 'because it simply wasn't practical for everyone to get involved'. The group was selected according to its strengths, experience and desire to make it happen. Excellent.

Except this was School with Pay.

- 10 weeks out from the event date, we held a one-hour 'kick-off' conference call to convene as a group and agree the objectives of the offsite, we had three weeks to pull some core ideas together. (11 managers x 1 hour = 11 hours)

  🕐 ROLLING TOTAL = 11 hours

- We held three weekly, hour-long conference calls, to discuss ideas and brainstorm options for the event, alongside

  (Continued)

additional conversations and emails that went on behind the scenes. (11 managers x 1 hour x 3 phone calls = 33 hours)

🕐 **ROLLING TOTAL = 44 hours**

- We'd also organized smaller gatherings to progress specific areas in between each weekly call. (11 managers x 2 hours x 3 weeks = 66 hours)

🕐 **ROLLING TOTAL = 110 hours**

- We then held a two-day planning meeting at the venue. Day 1 was to finalize the high level design of the event, with Day 2 dedicated to detailed planning and agreeing individual actions. (11 managers x 8 hours x 2 days = 176 hours, plus travel, 11 hotel rooms and 11 evening meals)

🕐 **ROLLING TOTAL = 286 hours**

We were five weeks out from the offsite. After five weeks of discussions, conference calls and activity, we had a plan. We'd agreed a budget and we all had our actions. We were in good shape. At least 286 combined hours, or nearly 36 man-days of effort had got us to this point.

And then the school bell rang.

- Just *one* week after our two-day planning session, a couple of senior stakeholders asked in a meeting for an update on the conference plan. They then raised some concerns over the flow of the event and suggested new and additional content they'd like to see in the already full schedule. They wanted a re-think and also reduced the budget significantly. (6 people x 1 hour discussion = 6 hours)

🕐 **ROLLING TOTAL = 292 hours**

We were back in Assembly and these two executives had become Teachers. Having given our working group 'full responsibility', they were now marking our homework. The process had become an enormous See Me. To make things worse, some members of the working group instantly became like students, who wouldn't answer back and instead did what they were told, because due to their seniority, the Teachers knew best.

Rather than interacting with their stakeholders and re-stating the governance that had been agreed upfront to avoid this sort of scenario, they simply followed the Teachers, and rushed off to the naughty corner to redo their homework, emailing the working group late that night, to say that the agenda would 'have to be reworked'.

- Meanwhile, a number of other meetings and conference calls were already taking place to progress specific areas of previously agreed actions, with the input of other people across the business, who were blissfully unaware of two people's request for rework. (11 managers x 4 meetings x 2 hours = 88 hours)

🕐 **ROLLING TOTAL** = **380 hours**

Tired yet?

- A conference call was held two days later. The first 30 minutes was spent discussing the budget and event costs (which had already been done in the two-day planning session) and the second 30 minutes was spent discussing the requests for additional agenda items from the senior stakeholder meeting (which had already been done in the two-day planning session). Our conclusions were the same, but we were over-ruled. (9 people x 1 hour = 9 hours)

🕐 **ROLLING TOTAL** = **389 hours**

(Continued)

We were four weeks out: the 'working group with full authority' had worked on the offsite for almost 400 hours, plus individual travel costs and other unknown email and phone call time.

SCHOOL, WITH PAY.

300 hours. Until your homework gets marked.

Another 100 hours, because we're all scared of the Teachers.

400 hours. Almost 50 man-days of effort. And our work was back on our desks, covered in red marker pen.

The conference was forgettable.

I use this example not because it's extreme, but simply because it's *not*. This sort of scenario is probably familiar to many of us and is likely being repeated in teams, divisions and entire organizations across the working planet if they have School with Pay directing their thinking.

It could have been 50 days invested in team culture, support and celebration, with a working party able to work cross-border, cross-job roles and play to their strengths not the structure chart. Instead, it was 50 days *wasted*.

Four hundred hours. Fifty days. And if it could happen there, it's probably being repeated, in countless others meetings and projects and at a cultural and financial cost that's probably unfathomable.

It's not about the right of senior people to make decisions and exert their authority. It's about 50 days wasted because of *poor ways of working*.

And yet none of us have any time and we all say we're busy.

The story above is not a corporate disaster, no-one was injured and the failure I've described will never be reported in the national press. In fact, no-one other than the people involved will ever even know about it.

And that's the problem. Time management failure is an unseen problem, not significant enough to alert the radar, not impactful enough when we're 'staying out of trouble' to ever be engaged with … and so it will happen again and be replicated and repeated across the hundreds and thousands of people who are silently working in a School with Pay environment, complaining about their schedules and yet every day creating inefficiencies.

No-one has any time, yet School with Pay always wastes it.

If you're running School with Pay, do the maths.

If you're playing the student or reverting to Teacher, break out your calculator. The numbers might scare you.

We rarely have enough time between us and when we're not at our MOST, we'll likely have even less of it.

Six Bricks

The final aspect in more effectively managing the time we have is in who we spend it with. If it's true that we become like those we surround ourselves with, the company we keep will demand regular attention.

Think about the way the bricks are arranged to construct an effective wall, as in Figure 8.

Let's pick one of the bricks in the wall (Figure 9).

In any well-built wall, each individual brick is surrounded by six others (Figure 10).

Six Bricks is a simple model for reviewing the company you keep and the impact it has on your thinking and performance.

Think about the six people or 'bricks' who are surrounding you in the work you do. This isn't just the six people you might spend

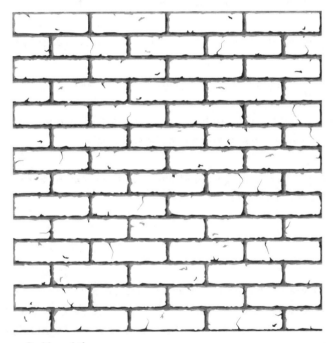

Figure 8: Your Life

the most time with; it's also those who have the greatest influence over you and your thinking – the people you've 'let in'. The words of the people we've let into our minds should matter to us, because they words they say are influential, directional and high impact.

Note down your six bricks. If you want, you could consider the outer layer of the additional 12 bricks and capture their names as well.

Now grade each brick in terms of that person's impact on you. Give them a score of 1 to 10 for how positive their influence is

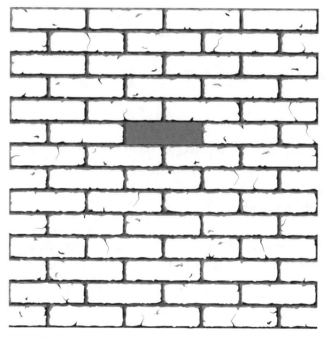

Figure 9: You

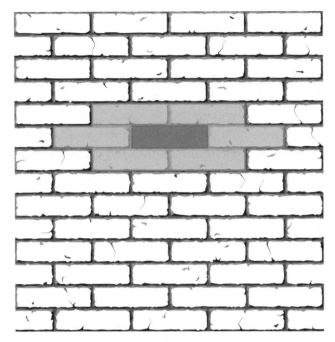

Figure 10: You and Your Six Bricks

on you and the overall effect of them being in your wall (1 = less positive, 10 = more positive).

What do you notice?

- How well are the people that you're surrounding yourself with helping you in your thinking and to what extent is their presence in your working life and schedule working for you?
- Are there some gaps, or some bricks that need filling?
- Are there people who are important to you, but where you're not seeing or hearing enough of them?

We do ultimately become like the people we surround ourselves with. And just like apps updating, the bricks in our individual walls can and should be adjusted over time. There are people who played a significant part in my life and schedule in times past whose influence I realized had become less than helpful. There were voices that I discovered had stopped having a positive impact on me, or had become outdated and were no longer helping me grow. At various times in my life, I've chosen to rebuild the wall of the people I allow to have a significant influence in my life. And while many of the bricks I've removed might be people I'm still in contact with, they wouldn't now form one of my six critical bricks or even the additional twelve who make up the outer layer. There are also times when there wouldn't be six, but maybe two or three that are critically important to me.

I'm more selective than ever about the people I spend my time with and in particular those who I 'let in' to my thinking. My bricks feed my mindset and influence my thinking, which is far too important to leave to chance or politeness. And as ever and always, updates to the bricks around us and the people who influence us are available if we need them.

- Who are the bricks surrounding you at the moment?
- How is your wall working and what changes might be necessary?
- Review your schedule – are you spending enough time with the right sorts of people? Are the right sorts of voices the ones that you're listening to?

When our priorities are effectively organized, we begin to take seriously the outworking of our schedules. When we give consideration to the people we're spending our too-precious Time with and make conscious decisions to be with people who'll be of benefit to us, I believe our Mindsets will grow stronger, our Outcomes will get attention and our Strengths can be more effectively manifested.

And when *that* starts to happen, we'll find ourselves Showing Up just like we did in our interview.

NOW SHOW UP!

We've looked at five all new, hugely powerful and empowering working paradigms.

A reimagined sense of the work you do, where you **Think, Create, Believe, Connect** and where your foundational starting point is that **All is Well**.

- You have a dialled-in **Mindset** that's brimming with confidence.
- You have compelling **Outcomes** that are thought through and well-formed.
- You've discovered your **Strengths** and are committed to developing and applying them.

And all this is reflected in a schedule that makes the most of your **Time** and is disciplined in maximizing it.

Who'd ever be able to stop you, if you really started working like that?

When You're Showing Up, Everything Shows Up With You.

At the end of 2008, when I'd decided to start my own company, I was naturally concerned about finances. With a family and a mortgage, I had responsibilities that were significant and at times found my thinking clouded by fears of possible failure and the not-so-helpful and unsolicited remarks of those worried about the market and the impact of the evolving economic downturn.

At the same time, I'd embarked on a development programme, where we regularly watched film clips and discussed their content. It was on this programme that I discovered the work of Benjamin Zander, conductor of the Boston Philharmonic Orchestra, regular speaker on the application of the orchestra in leadership and business and the author of the bestselling *The Art of Possibility* with his partner Rosamund Zander.

As we sat watching *The Conducting Business*, a biographical short film made in 1996, I was stopped in my tracks by a throwaway line towards the end of one of his presentations. He was addressing a group of UK business people and as he so often does, encouraging them to reveal their inner musician and allow their performance to shine, in what he describes brilliantly as 'one-buttock playing'.[1] Zander focuses on the Contribution of all of us, as a game in which 'you wake up each day and bask in the notion that you are a gift to others'.

As he leapt around the stage, he told another story:

> '...the president of a company once said to me, "I like contribution, but you have to make money!" And I said, "you know that's

---

[1] There are a number of Benjamin Zander talks available online, but his TED talks are among my favourites and in this one you'll get to observe one-buttock playing in action: http://www.ted.com/talks/benjamin_zander_on_music_and _passion.html.

the funny thing about money; it sort of shows up
...around contribution, money shows up.'

The Money Shows Up.

It was as though the four words had been stamped on my fore-head. I knew in that moment that my focus hadn't been on my Contribution; the things I was good at and how the company I was launching would help people, support them and through our work make a difference.'

Contribution is a factor of what for me has become Showing Up, and it's now about far more than my relationship with money. Over the last few years, as I've worked with the MOST model and integrated it in my own life and commercial activity, it's underlined the value of Showing Up in its fullness and how a shift in attention can make a whole world of difference.

Whether it's money, or outcomes, or clients or career plan, when we Show Up, I think *it* shows up, I think *they* show up and in fact, *it all* shows up. Where our attention is, is where we'll go. And Showing Up means operating at our MOST and when we start doing that, the world spins along with us.

Our Mindset, our Outcomes and the application of our Strengths in the work we do lays the foundation for the performance we'll deliver. And the quality of our performance will be manifested in how and where we spend our Time and what we ultimately manage to do with it. Giving attention to these four aspects of our working experience means we've left School with Pay and spend more time Showing Up at our MOST.

We shake off old paradigms, remove our elasticated ties and begin to take some well-needed control.

When we operate at our MOST, School with Pay is **History**.

When we operate at our MOST, everything starts **Showing Up**.

Less School. More Purpose.

Less Fear. More Confidence.

Less Power-Loss. More Belief.

Less Control. More Responsibility.

Less Game-playing. Far more Fun.

Less Hiding. More Showing Up.

Update Now?

Well, at least you knew *this* question was coming.

My hope is that each of the preceding chapters have in some way served to pause your working hamster wheel, disrupt what might have been previously fixed ways of thinking and provoke an Update in your perspective on the work you do. New ways of operating and framing the professional lives we lead *are* possible if we choose to embrace them and give the Showing Up paradigms the space and opportunity to transform our working mindset and performance.

This entire book has been an Update; an Invitation with a Purpose. And it begs a few questions:

- What new version of you is now ready to emerge in tomorrow's workplace?
- Where has your thinking been refreshed, for the person you're becoming?
- What will Showing Up look like for you; in your thinking, in your workplace and with your colleagues and your customers?
- What are the small changes and practical actions you'll take, that from this point forward will reduce the water around your Iceberg and mean we see more of you in the world on a more regular basis?
- What does You Version 2.0 look like, and who are you going to tell about it?

Take some time to think this through. Yep. Now. We'll wait. This is important.

A few more questions to help you form your own thinking.

If you were asked to describe the bubbling updates in your thinking and what Showing Up for you might look like when you head back to the office, what would you say?

- What are the improvements that you're about to make to your performance?
- What glitches have you ironed out or what bugs have you resolved for yourself?
- What have you uncovered, that's been buried under the water but will now be on view, as you Back Yourself as an individual and Show Up in all your power?

- Where will you stop playing Student?
- Where will you quit playing Teacher?

Look back, think back and reflect on where you've got to.

Your working life might be about to change forever.

Updates Are Available. Always. For all of us. And as ever and as I promised you, there's an important further step to take. It's whispered, it's patient and it's the thing that's all important:

Update Now?

A Warning Call

DJ Shadow wrote a song called 'Warning Call' on his 2001 album *The Less You Know, The Better* where he takes a swipe at the messages we were taught at school, with a reminder that 'it's cool to be you, when you like what you do'.

Showing Up could be one of your greatest achievements in life, because it flings open the doors of possibility, with a renewed positivity and a powerful presence you might never have thought possible. Imagine working where you no longer give power to others, but where you take your place in the world, planting your feet firmly and confidently and beginning to make the most of every working opportunity.

School with Pay is full of people swimming in circles.

Leaving School means it really *is cool* to be you. It's always cool to be you, when you like what you do. And with five new paradigms you're Strong. Headstrong.

Showing Up is the very best sort of Warning Call.

To the world, to get ready for you.

And to you from yourself; a compelling reminder to never again be a diminished version of yourself through the way you frame the work you do or to reduce the value of your place in the world while you're doing it.

The Last Day of Term

Today is the final day of your personal last term and school is *Over*. It's time for us all to get our shirts signed by our school mates and exit the gates with graffiti-covered backs. Today, **YOU** leave School and head out into a world that's waiting for you. Today marks the point where you start Showing Up at a whole new level, and where you'll discover there's plenty of room and capacity for you to make your presence felt.

Today you leave the registration room for the very last time. So you can throw away your pencil case, burn your school tie and rip up your timetable ... because there's a new world on offer once you put down your school bag.

Get yourself ready, because this particular Iceberg's getting ready to Show Up even more potently than it did in an interview.

Why not *you*?

Why not *now*?

And where does this story finish? I don't know, because right now it's just a possibility. Your apps are still developing. Like every game-changing update, it starts with an invitation and an open offer to every last one of us.

So we're only getting started.

The final destination of Showing Up is unclear, but it's a new direction of travel and an option that's compelling us. Where we take Showing Up from here is down to each of us, pressing into our own responses, with the impact we'll deliver and the stories we'll tell others, when we occasionally look back up the mountain and see how far our fresh attention has taken us.

Showing Up is like Fight Club, except you can join without the bruising. Right now it's an idea, a concept to engage with and as members we'll begin to define it (somehow, maybe ...).

The first rule of Showing Up is ... you tell *everyone* about Showing Up.

And the second rule of Showing Up is **You Tell Everyone About Showing Up**.

Ready? Then let's go.

See you out there sometime.

Now Show Up!!

Sign your school shirt and continue the conversation at www.nowshowup.com
#NowShowUp

ABOUT TIM ROBSON

Before launching his training and consultancy practice, Tim Robson was Head of Service Design for Marks and Spencer, where he worked across all store formats, sales channels and product lines and developed performance and brand programmes for stores and remote teams.

Tim's passion to coach and develop teams started early in his career with Prudential, where after project and operational roles, he left as Head of UK Business Improvement. As described in *Showing Up*, he also took a formative career break in the mid-90s to become a youth worker, run a skate park and take teams of young people to Africa to support community projects.

Tim's leadership experience is supported by his ongoing study of communication, people and team behaviour and his own development as an NLP Master Practitioner. A runner, cyclist and Tour de France fanatic, he now lives with his family in Stratford on Avon, although remains entirely unable to quote Shakespeare effectively.

nowshowup.com

ACKNOWLEDGEMENTS

Showing Up has been a journey that wouldn't have been possible without some very important people.

Firstly, to Jonathan, Jenny and the fab team at Capstone. Thank you all, for 'getting it' and for your support in getting this project over the line.

To my clients and colleagues and anyone who's listened to me. Thanks for providing valuable material (!) and for being open to these new ways of thinking. Now. Show. Up!!

To Jo, my great PA – thank you for arriving so seamlessly and creating the space for me to get it all finished on time – ta!

To Pierre and Dana, my two international bricks, I thank you; Pierre for believing in the concept from the outset and Dana for being there and saying 'Why don't you?'

To Dad for bringing that old phone home and to Mum for providing the stationery – who knew, eh?!

And finally to Steph, Jack and Lucy. You three are simply brilliant. Thanks for putting up with the absences, distractions and silences and for giving me space in the times when I've needed it. Your patience is remarkable and I don't deserve any of you. Well, maybe I do. See you on the slopes sometime.

INDEX